*To all friends of Abbot Hall*

*William Green*
*of*
*Ambleside*

*William Green (from H. D. Rawnsley, By Fell and Dale)*

# *William Green*
# *of*
# *Ambleside*

## A LAKE DISTRICT ARTIST
## (1760 — 1823)

# M. E. Burkett and J. D. G. Sloss

Abbot
Hall
ART GALLERY

KENDAL·CUMBRIA

ISBN 09503335 4 9


1st Published April 1984

Published by Abbot Hall Art Gallery, Kendal, Cumbria
Printed by W.G. Print, Kendal, Cumbria.

# Contents

# *Preface*

This book is really the result of a fortuitous but chance meeting at Abbot Hall a few years ago with Mr. Purves from Melbourne. First he told me we had a nice William Green picture. Being in a hurry for a meeting, I answered in the affirmative and prepared to go, when he added, "I have one at home." I grunted, but before I could leave he said, "I'm his great, great, great grandson." I stood still and he said, "I have his diaries at home and do not know what to do with them." I missed the meeting! The diaries arrived a few weeks later by surface mail and since then, alas, the donor has died.

Ever since working in Ambleside in 1954 I have been interested in William Green, and the pride with which the locals viewed him, but it was not until I met an enthusiastic collector of his work — David Sloss — that the idea of a book and an exhibition developed: for the latter, David Sloss was kind enough to offer his collection of Green's work. It was after doing the research and writing the original chapters in collaboration with David, and especially in connection with the chapter on Art, that we felt an editor was needed, and happily Christopher Gowan undertook the task of tidying up the manuscript, thus greatly improving it. Then we needed an artist who was actively engaged in print-making to write about Green's etchings, and Donald Wilkinson kindly agreed to do a chapter on this aspect of his work. We were very happy when Norman Nicholson, the poet agreed to write the Introduction. Finally, to go with the publication, it was agreed it was essential to have an exhibition of William Green's work, and this has been arranged from April to June 1984 at Abbot Hall: it will then go to three other venues; Middlesborough, Keighley, and Dove Cottage, Grasmere.

Though not a Turner or a Constable, Green certainly seems due for a little attention.

M. E. BURKETT

# *Acknowledgements*

Grateful thanks go to many people who have helped with the book and with the exhibition. Lenders will not be mentioned by name, but their help is very much appreciated. Thanks are due to the British Museum, Mr. H. V. Wilkinson for all his help and generous loans, Dove Cottage Grasmere, Manchester City Art Gallery, the Victoria & Albert Museum and to the Armitt Library, for loans and photographs included in the exhibition.

For help in typing, proof-reading and research we are indebted to Mrs. E. Jay, Miss H. A. Cummins, Madame Monique Choinard, Mrs. Handley, Robert Walker, Adam Naylor, Miss C. A. Moorby, Mrs. O. M. Rummens and Miss V. A. J. Slowe. For help with photography we are grateful to Leslie Randall. Finally we remember with gratitude Green's great, great, great grandson, Mr. J. R. W. Purves, through whom it all started.

We are most grateful to the following people for their generous financial help towards the publication of this book:- Provincial Insurance PLC, Curwen Archives Trust, Paul Mellon Foundation, Granton Investments Ltd., and to Manchester Corporation for a small contribution.

M. E. BURKETT

# Introduction

The work of William Green marks a turning-point in the way people looked at the Lakes. Before his time, artists such as William Gilpin came in search of 'The Picturesque' — of a view that would look good in a picture. Topographical accuracy was of little importance. Their models were Poussin, Claude and Salvator Rosa: their literary inspiration came from writers such as Thomas Gray, Thomas Pennant, William Hutchinson and Anne Radcliffe. Their exhilaration, the sense of discovery and the excited exaggerations of the 18th century had worked themselves out by Green's day.

Green, too, catered for the visitors. His *Tourist's New Guide,* published in 1819, was the first of the Highways-and-Byeways type of book in the Lakes, leading the traveller up every dale and over every pass. He drew a good deal from Fr. Thomas West's earlier *Guide to the Lakes,* but he is much more pedestrian than West, less concerned with the aesthetic and antiquarian aspects of landscape. His book is illustrated with aquatints, printed in a rather unpleasant mixture of brown and blue-green, which makes them seem far more old-fashioned — positively Gilpinesque! — than they must have been in the originals.

Green's *Guide* preceded the publication of Wordsworth's by several years, though the latter had appeared, in an earlier form, in 1810, as the anonymous Introduction to a volume of terribly bad drawings by the Rev. Joseph Wilkinson. That Introduction, of course, is a still unsurpassed essay on the general characteristics of the Lake District. In subsequent printings it was enlarged by extra material until, by 1842, when it was incorporated into what is now known as *Hudson's Guide,* it included the poet's own "Information for Tourists", together with articles on geology and botany, and a number of "Itineraries and admeasurements of distances."

Green's drawings are the visual equivalent of the change of attitude which can be seen from the additions to Wordsworth's original text, a change, it might be said, from the general to the particular. Looked at from the distance of nearly two hundred years, it may be seen as the first sign of a movement from fantasy to fact, from the subjective to the objective, from the exploratory to the conservationist, from the aesthetic to the scientific, from William Gilpin to William Rollinson.

Visitors to the exhibition at Abbot Hall Art Gallery, Kendal (27 April — 24 June 1984), will have had a chance to see Green's original work but, at the moment, I am more concerned with the two volumes of drawings which he published in 1809 and 1814 — and particularly with the latter. Green's technique here is that of using heavy black strokes for the foreground, lighter strokes for the middle distance, while the background is sketched comparatively faintly. This is an obvious way of suggesting perspective but, at least in the prints, it makes the background, which is usually that of the fells, look misty and indeterminate.

Now the main effect is to throw our interest much more on to the foreground, and this was something new in Lake District art. Gilpin and most of his contemporaries constructed their central landscape and then neatly framed it with 'side-screens' and 'fore-screens'. Any sort of tree or cow or block of stone would do so long as it set off the main subject. Green's foregrounds, on the other hand, are carefully observed and recorded. You feel that, for almost the first time, an artist has really looked at the rocks around him. His boulders do look like lumps of Cumbrian slate. His drawing of, say, Wallabarrow Crag, in the Duddon valley - not, by the way, the most hackneyed of subjects - gives the feeling of that wonderful fracas - rocks split from the crags, carried down by glaciers, tossed around by torrents, worn smooth by the continual abrasion and massage of running water. His walls and bridges and farms seem to be built of the stone on which they stand. I am not trying to argue that this kind of factual verisimilitude is necessarily the sign of a great artist. Green does not come into that category: but he made people look at what was really there. He was a corrective to the often absurd exaggerations and over-blown affectations of many of his predecessors and even some of his successors.

"What are men to rocks and mountains?", exclaimed Elizabeth Bennet, in *Pride and Prejudice,* when she learned that she might be going to visit the Lakes. William Green, at least in his pictures, showed no great interest in men, but his rocks were a good deal more real and solid than any that Miss Bennet would have been expecting to see.

NORMAN NICHOLSON

way between thence &
Ewes Mere, & on to the
common —— is there
any good view of Ulls
Water on the way from
Powley Bridge on the
Westmorland ride to
Penrith — all about
Lyulphs Tower, Glen
coin & Glenridden
must be examined
and the down views
from the head of the
lake — but from the
round beginning at Blea
Wyke & coming down

*Page from William Green's Diary*

*Brantrigg Gill.*

# Chapter 1

# Early Travellers to the Lake District

As early as in the 16th Century, Camden wrote about the scenery of the Lake District, with its "bunching rocks and pretty hills", but it was another two centuries before this scenery became generally admired. In 1698 Celia Fiennes records in her "Journeys" that she visited Windermere, but the object of the visit was not only to view the scenery but to taste the Windermere char, a fish already so famous that, for instance, James Graham of Levens Hall used to order his steward to send down potted char to London, where he presented some to Queen Anne. Plenty of people skirted the area: in 1730 Whitehaven was said to be the third busiest port in England, after London and Bristol. The Lowther mines round Workington had made their owner the "richest commoner in England"; and Appleby School was so good that George Washington's brothers were sent there from Virginia to be educated, and he very nearly followed them himself. Kendal had long been the second most important wool town in the country: Carlisle was the biggest town in the Border Marches. But all these were peripheral.

In 1645 Howells spoke of mountains as "enormous monstrous excrescences of nature". In 1712 Blackmore referred to them as "the shame and heavy burden of the earth". Defoe described the Lake District as "the wildest and most frightful", and as late as 1767 John Brown of Penrith condemned the Lake and Vale of Keswick for their "horrible grandeur — steep and shaggy sides, dreadful heights, rude and terrible magnificence". But already a change of attitude had begun, springing from Rousseau's *Nouvelle Heloise*, published in 1761. He wrote: "It is a general impression which all men experience, though not all notice it, that on high mountains, where the air is pure and subtle, one feels a lightness in the body, a serenity of spirit: pleasures are there less ardent, passions are tempered".

After the publication of the *Nouvelle Heloise* and *Emile* (1762), the cult of romantic landscape spread over Western Europe. Thomas Gray passing Thirlmere in 1769 said "I now began to see Helm Crag — stones in wild confusion"; but he concluded "all is peace, rusticity and happy poverty", a phrase which might come straight from Rousseau. By 1802 Charles and Mary Lamb came, and he said "great floundering bears and mountains appeared couchant — that which tourists find romantic". And that there were tourists is shown by Jane Austen in *Pride and Prejudice,* published finally in 1813 but mainly written in 1796: in it Elizabeth Bennet is invited by her aunt and uncle to accompany them to the Lakes, and exclaims: "My dear, dear aunt, what delight! What felicity! . . . What are men to rocks and mountains? Oh, what hours of transport we shall spend! And when we *do* return, it shall not be like other travellers, without being able to give one accurate idea of anything. We *will* know where we have gone . . . Lakes, mountains and rivers shall not be jumbled together in our imaginations; nor, when we attempt to describe any particular scene, will we begin quarrelling about its relative situation".

These tourists needed guides and guide books, and both became available. Hutton was the chief guide for the Royal Oak Hotel at Ambleside, and all other hotels had guides. Mr. Partridge was a guide for the Salutation Inn for over 40 years. The best Guide Book was written by Thomas West, who was born in about 1717 and went to school in Edinburgh. Thence he went to the English School at St. Omer before entering the priesthood. He was a brilliant scholar, and lived for some time at "Titeup Hall," Dalton. He died at Sizergh Castle, and was buried in the Strickland family chapel in Kendal Church in 1779.

At the turn of the century William and Dorothy Wordsworth began to extol the beauties of the area. They were joined by Southey, and for some years by Samuel Taylor Coleridge, and these "Lake Poets", as they became known after 1817, make the Lakes a totally acceptable place.

Among all these famous names there is one who knew them all, and who perhaps in his own way did as much as they to popularize, and incidentally to record, the Lake District at the turn of the century. They only wrote about the district. William Green felt impelled to write too, and in 1819 produced *The Tourist's New*

*Guide to the English Lake District*. But he did much more than write: he drew it and painted it. In 1795 he published *Forty-eight views of the Lake District and Four Views of Wales*, and in 1796 a *Series of picturesque views of the North of England*. Indeed it is perhaps a pity that he did not take his own advice, after writing in the New Guide "for the author of the present work might with greater ease, and probably with more advantage to himself, have worked up for the amusement of the eye a number of drawings and paintings during the time he has been engaged in this matter of mere utility".

Yet he had in fact already produced "a number of drawings and paintings". His 19th C. biographer Charles Roeder tentatively puts it at 1000 finished pictures; and the constant flow of visitors to his annual exhibitions in Ambleside and Keswick must have been responsible for carrying his work all over Britain. He had a host of admirers up and down the country, including such subscribers as His Majesty's Library, and figures such as H. R. H. The Prince Regent, the Archduke of Austria, Lord Dalhousie, Lord Clifford, the Rt. Hon. the Earl of Lonsdale and John Dalton.

In addition to individual works, he had published series of *Studies from Nature* every year or two from 1804 onwards, and he continued this work till his death in 1823. In the 1819 Guidebook he writes

"The Old Halls, Farm Houses and Cottages of the North of England have long been admired for their elegant pecularity of design, and, aided by accidental additions and delapidations, and by combinations of the richest woods, and back-grounds of rocks and mountains, are, in their kind, finer objects for study than any others to be met with in the island.

"Modernizing has, however, recently spoiled many of these buildings, and a few years more will probably see them pared and plaistered into all the monotony of the erections of the present day.

"To save from the wreck of time and the busy hand of man ("man out of his place") the best specimens of this mountain architecture, by a series of representations, on a scale adequate to their beauty and importance, has long been the wish of the writer, who, for such a purpose, has already proposed to publish

| | |
|---|---|
| 30 Views of Abbeys | 5 guineas |
| 30 Views of Castles, Old Halls & Farm Houses | 5 guineas |
| 30 Views of English Lakes | 5 guineas |
| 30 Views of Mountains, Rivers, Waterfalls, etc | 5 guineas" |

Hartley Coleridge said of Green "Amid many discouragements and with no better patrons than the mutable public of Lakers, his spirit never flagged, his hand and eye were never idle, and he had a healthy love for his employment such as none but an honest man could understand."

From a study of his subscribers' lists, it is clear how popular they were. Southey was the first to subscribe to his etchings of 1813, paying £1-5-0, and on the same list are three members of the Lloyd family, including Charles. Lloyds, Southeys and Wordsworths appeared on most subscribers' lists with great regularity. Wordsworth was a great admirer and regular subscriber: he was first on the list for 40 small views etched from nature. And a note in Green's Diary of 1817 shows "6th Dec. Colouring the four drawings James Newton and Dolly Wordsworth".

Even in the early '50's of this century, people of the Ambleside area would show with pride prints by William Green of Ambleside. Now, alas, it is some of the "off-comers" who collect and prize his work, mostly his paintings: perhaps this is fitting, since for all his 23 years of residence at Ambleside, (he was 40 when he moved there) he was an "off-comer" himself. The days of the popularity of black and white etchings waned at the turn of this century: the demand was filled by photographic views, first in black and white and then in colour.

His work, to be discussed in a later chapter, was very uneven. Some of it, though, rises well above mediocrity; and the part he played in popularising the Lake District was unquestionable. Wordworth's tribute to him on his gravestone was well merited.

# Chapter 2

# William Green's Life

The only account of William Green's life came at the end of the 19th century and was written by Charles Roeder.[1] When Roeder began he found very little material and much that was written erroneously, even in the Dictionary of National Biography. The *Manchester Mercury,* collected in 16 volumes, covering 1779—1796, proved very helpful. Green's contributions to extracts from that form an autobiographical record. At the time of writing Roeder found Mr. W. H. Mayson, a surviving grandson of William Green in Manchester, who provided much material about Green. Roeder portrayed him as "an unassuming toiler"; "His comprehensive knowledge of the Lakes stood above that of all the men of his time, not excepting Wordsworth".

His life can be divided into 3 periods — his childhood, and work in Manchester as a surveyor 1760-95; his stay in London, from 1796-99/1800; and the final period in Ambleside, from 1800-1823.

He was the son of Joshua Green (b. 1725) by his father's first wife Catherine Simpson, whom he had married on 22nd February 1756, and who died on 5th September 1760 in her 27th year, just eleven days after giving birth to her son William on the 25th August. They lived at 3 Windmill Street, Lad Lane, Deansgate, where William was born. Joshua acted as clerk of St. John's Church, Deansgate, with the rector, the Rev. John Clowes. Joshua married, for the second time at the same church, Elizabeth Hartley, and William soon had a half-brother, Bernard Hartley Green, who died on 16th August 1820. Hartley became a cotton merchant and an early Chairman of the Manchester Exchange and borough-reve of Salford.

William was taught by his father, a schoolmaster from Northamptonshire, and inherited his good writing. He did not go to the Grammar School, as has been stated elsewhere; but he did go to Dr. Henry Clarke's mathematical school in Salford, answering four mathematical questions in 1775, and three the following year. He showed early promise in geometry and drawing. Dr. Clarke had himself been a surveyor in the town in 1765: he also cultivated the art of perspective drawing, examples of which can be seen in the plans he drew for Whitaker's *History of Manchester* of 1765 and 1771.

Throughout his life, as in his diaries he later recorded, Green made visits back to Manchester to visit his relatives. From 1776-7 he went from Dr. Clarke to Christopher Woodroofe, a local surveyor and planner. His teachers were vastly impressed by his work, and drew the attention of William Yates of Liverpool to him in order to help Yates with his projected survey of the County Palatine of Lancaster. So it was that at 18, from 1778-9, William went to "Lancashire-north-of-the-Sands", and he loved it. From there he had his first real glimpse of the Lake District and fell in love with the area, about a quarter of which was in Lancashire until 1974. Yates began to survey in 1778 and finished in 1787. Green was evidently helping to sell it for Yates in Manchester, as Harrop's *Mercury,* December 12th 1787, p.1906 says, "subscribers may be supplied also by Mr. Green, Manchester, who was an assistant in this work". Green referred to these days later as a very happy part of his life.

In Green's *Tourist's New Guide* 1819, p.4. he says "The writer was encouraged to the pursuit of painting by Mr. West, but why he knows not, his few sketches were humble, his mind untutored, and he knew none of the requisite theories, but geometry, perspective and architecture".

It was on a visit to Ulverston that he first met Thomas West, who was working on his historical and topographical work on the area. West's Guide was published in 1778 following *Antiquities of Furness* in 1774, and he was by then well-known. Green was greatly encouraged by West's suggestion that he should become an artist himself, and soon after going back to Manchester began taking painting lessons.

In the Furness area his eyes had been opened to the beauties of nature and he wished to portray it all. In Manchester in 1779 "he acquaints the gentlemen of the town etc. that he practises the art of

Land Surveying, as measuring and planning estates, setting out land for building on, dividing of ground, levelling etc." The following year, in 1780, "he is returned from finishing the survey of the County of Lancaster for Wm. Yates, of Liverpool, and therefore at leisure to pursue his own employment of measuring and planning estates ... His terms of land survey and planning are: Estate measuring and mapping 1/- per square acre, measuring land for the content only, six pence per statute acre; for finishing any old plan of estate in the new method, six pence per statute acre, and six pence for every mile the estate lies distant from Manchester (as it is necessary to inspect every field, as plowed, pasture, and meadow are differently distinguished, as likewise the fences, whether hedges, walls, cops, dykes, or pales, as likewise hilly ground, etc.; levelling, dividing, etc., according to the time and trouble)." His progress was such that by 1783 he had so excelled that he was asked to teach the subject.

In 1783 "returning thanks to those gentlemen who have been pleased to employ him with surveying, drawing etc." he announced that a school would be opened at the corner of Tassel Street, near Ridgefield, for the instruction of young gentlemen, in the arts of drawing and painting. "Ladies and gentlemen may see a great variety of his performances at this school, which he'll regularly attend from 2-4 and 6-8 in order to teach." This was probably West's advice after returning from Furness. William Marshall Craig, a miniaturist of Manchester, may also have influenced him to do so, as he was a close friend. His enterprise did not stop here and in 1786 he advertised to the public that he had opened another school for ladies, "at his house at 2 Brazenose Street in drawing, writing and accounts, ladies and gentlemen instructed at home and boarding schools attended as usual."

At this time, 1786, he must have determined to undertake a full survey of Manchester. Much development was taking place and the old landmarks were fast disappearing, so he realised it must be done with some urgency. There were some plans in existence and he studied old maps by R. Casson and J. Berry, which had appeared last in 1757 before the copper plates for them had been taken over by Harrop. Apart from these, a small and inadequate map had been made in 1772 by T. Tinker, junior, called *A Plan of Manchester & Salford*. Green was fully qualified to meet the challenge of preparing a new comprehensive and up-to-date map and he also was fully familiar with the whole area. He sounded people out and found the responses favourable, so he set about to prepare the finest survey to have been carried out on Manchester up to that time and indeed up to the time of Charles Roeder's article, late in the 19th century.

He set out his plans in full with intentions to draw in subscribers to the work.

"Prospects for publishing, by subscription, a plan of the town of Manchester and Salford, to be drawn from an actual survey of Wm. Green.
It is proposed in this plan to lay down all the streets, squares, spaces, courts, lanes, yards, passages, fields, gardens, etc., etc., in such a manner as to express the exact dimensions of every regularly bounded plot of land in the township of Manchester and Salford, that will fall within that square which shall be judged the most proper to encompass it. Upon the unbuilt land will be specified all the intended improvements, for which purpose plans of the intended streets will be requested from the owners.
The Plan will be laid down upon the scale of 40 or 50 yards to an inch, — at present it cannot well be determined which will be the most eligible. The drawings will be made in a modern and approved style, and when finished, will be submitted to the inspection of the subscribers at large. From the proposed large extent of this plan, it will be engraved upon 4 copper-plates which will be executed by a good master.
The impressions will, with the strictest honour, be delivered in order as they are subscribed for, at one Guinea each.
The survey will be begun to be made, as soon as 500 copies are subscribed for, and it is eagerly requested that such as wish to become subscribers, will be as early as possible in signifying their names, that the proposer may embrace the opportunity of surveying all the streets this summer, which cannot be conveniently done after 7 o'clock in the morning, on account of the interruption of carriage.
Books for the reception of subscribers' names are open at J. Harrop's Printer, Mr. Matthew Falkner, and Mr Clarke's, in the Market Place, and at Wm. Green's, No. 2 Brazenose Street, who has now upon sale a valuable collection of Prints etc.
A number of respectable gentlemen in the town and neighbourhood of Manchester, being desirous that this plan shall include the whole of the township of Manchester and Salford, and as much of the adjoining townships, as will fall within that square, which will be formed from the extensions of the said two townships, Mr. Green hopes that this will be a sufficient apology for advancing the subscription to one guinea each copy."

Just a month later however, this great work was threatened by an advertisement in the *Mercury* which stated that another plan of Manchester & Salford was to be on the market and carried out by J. Oldham. In fact nothing came of this threat and there is no further reference to it. But five years later,

Green's Survey

in December 1791, a real threat appeared, in the sudden arrival of a Frenchman named Charles Laurent who was a cartographer. He was engaged in compiling fifty copper-plate views to illustrate a book, shortly to be published by the London firm of John Stockdale of Piccadilly, *A History of the County near Manchester.* Green had already spent so long on his maps, carefully recording every field and alley-way, that Laurent could see it was going to be a long task, and also that the end result would be large and quite expensive. He realised he could make a lot of money and a name for himself if he were to act swiftly and produce his maps before Green had time to complete his own. He had to find out how far Green had gone, and soon made himself known to him on the pretext of helping him. Green refused his help but Laurent had discovered all he needed to know. Poor Green wrote a desperate note in the *Mercury* of 13th December 1791 saying,

"Mr. Green finding it industriously circulated that he has entirely given up his intention of completing his survey, conceives himself for the liberal patronage he has experienced under the obligation of informing his subscribers that so far from relinquishing it, the Plan is three fourths finished, and that he intends laying aside all his other occupations to appropriate the ensuing half-year, from Christmas to midsummer, solely to that work, about which time, as part of it will very early in spring be put into the hands of able engravers, he hopes to complete it. From a plan, lately begun by another person who wished to assist Mr. Green, he hopes he shall not be injured in the public opinion, as the difference between a plan made from an actual survey, with accurate instruments, and conducted upon principles true in theory (which will be explained to every scientific enquirer) and one made by striding, is too palpable to escape observations."

Laurent, however, opened a subscription list for his maps in 1792. Green made another appeal in the *Mercury* in October 1793, saying that his plan would be ready in a few weeks; but it was not in fact published until late in 1794. It was drawn to a scale of sixty yards to one inch, or twenty nine inches to one mile. It showed the North at the top and measured, all nine large sheets, about eleven feet, nine inches by nine feet four inches. Laurent had drawn to a scale of seventeen inches to one mile and his only measured six feet by three feet two inches. There is a copy of Green's magnificent map at the Manchester Geographical Society. It was engraved by his old friend John Thornton, and bore a graceful vignette by his other friend, the miniaturist W. M. Craig, who had a studio in Manchester at the top of Market Street Lane. The quality of and information shown on the maps is a fitting tribute to his hours of work and recording and greatly valued in Manchester. In comparison, Laurent's was, according to Roeder, "a piece of plagiarism by a man who, backed up by Harrop and Stockdale's powerful influence managed to procure the aid of local surveyors and owners . . . His orientation is also done in the old style", whereas Green's was a scientific effort. Sadly, of course, Laurent's smaller map sold well while Green's was not a financial success; he only sold 400 out of the 600 copies. In fact, he still had some to offer for sale in Ambleside in 1819. Laurent was quick to take the opportunity of correcting his first impressions in several places after Green's maps were published and Charles Roeder is strong in his contempt. "This imposter played upon the credulity of the public, awe-struck with his powers, when he perambulated the town with chain and field book." Stockdale even went as far as praising Laurent for having surveyed, and a foreigner at that, without the knowledge of the language and "by eye alone . . . without the use of instruments and in the coldest part of the year . . . in less than two months two towns for some miles in circumference, with all their intricate communications." Faint praise for what was supposed to have been a serious scientific work!

So great had his concentration been on finishing the maps that Green had had little time to do anything else in those difficult years excepting for a brief visit to Buttermere in 1791, and in 1793 he went to Wales and the Lake District with his stalwart helper Thornton; but in 1794 he revisited Cumberland for twelve weeks, two of which were devoted to Buttermere. In 1795 came Green's first publication on the Lake District, the *Forty-eight Views of the Lake District and Four Views of Wales,* drawn and published by William Green. These he made as aquatints, and the next series followed in 1796 — *Series of Picturesque Views of the North of England,* where by 1796, the survey over, he informed the public that he was leaving behind his previous work and going to be a drawing master once again, but at 3 Lad Lane where he was again living with Hartley, his half-brother. This was not to last long however, for later in 1796 he wrote to all his friends and told them that he was going to live in London. After a brief exhibition in Manchester, he left to begin his career in the metropolis. His address was 74 Charlotte Street, Portland Place, and his friend Craig, who lived in London, was probably one of the influences in his going to London.

Apart from the fact that he moved among many of the leading artists of the day such as John Landseer, father of Sir Edwin Landseer, Robert Hills (1769-1844) one of the founders of the Society of Painters in Watercolours, and John Glover (1769-1844), we know little of his time there. He visited the Royal Academy, where he exhibited in 1797 and 1798, and frequented other exhibitions. One engraving by him at this period

*Richmond Bridge.*

was 'A View of Castle Street, Liverpool,' painted by Fernel. He practised engraving, etching, mezzotinting, and water colouring, all of which arts, according to Roeder, he had learnt in Manchester and not in London as had been thought by some. The British Museum's engraving of Derwentwater published by him in Manchester might have been done at the time of Yates' map-making after West's encouragement, but it is very poor.

One very important event in London was his marriage to Anne Bamford. He fell in love with Anne at first sight. She was fifteen years younger than he and fair with bright blue eyes. He was a tall man with flashing eyes and a ruddy complexion, who told his young bride that he would rather live on bread and water in that north country scenery than on the fat of the land in London. On 7th April 1799 their daughter Elizabeth was born. (She was to marry on 3rd February 1819 Mark Mayson of Keswick, and became the mother of W. H. Mayson of Manchester).

Despite all attempts to fulfil his artistic ideals by being in London and in contact with all the leading painters of the time, he found it strangely frustrating. He complained about the methods of art teaching of the day and the "mannerism" used. It caused him to question both, and to look back to nature for inspiration: "yet nature is invariable" he said. So, together with his engraving, etching and aquatinting materials and his pigments for colours which he always mixed carefully himself, it was in the summer of 1800 that he decided to go north (to the Lakes) to begin once again and to try to rid himself of all he had learnt over the last decade and "to adhere as faithfully as possible to nature".

Here again we find some confusion over dates and details: some biographers erroneously believed that he came North because of ill-health. Parson and White's *Gazeteer of Westmorland*, published in 1829 six years after his death, records him "residing some years at Keswick before settling in Ambleside", which cannot be true since he was certainly in London in the 1790's. In his own Lake District Guide Book he says he came to Ambleside in 1809, where "he took a House opposite the White Lion", and the etching showing his garden gate looking up to the Market Cross in its original position seems to support this site; but the date is clearly wrong.

He does appear to have looked carefully at various places, and in 1800 he settled in Ambleside. There he found considerable changes since his earlier visits, with Yates in 1778 and again in 1792 and 1794. Much of its picturesque quaintness had gone, but it still had a deep attraction for him. With his wife and daughter he took a small cottage in the Market Square, (adjacent to the Red Lion and opposite the White Lion), and there seven more children were born, though not all of them grew to maturity. The White Lion was the subject of one of his etchings. The Red Lion was an early name of The Queens.

There, in the twenty three remaining years of his life, he produced the main mass of his work relating to the area. He saw himself with almost missionary zeal as a recorder of his surroundings, so as to preserve a record of the remnants of antiquated rusticity which he remembered. With the same energy which had prompted him in his surveying, he set about recording the topography of the Lake District, from early morning till dusk. In the preface to his Guide he claims that "all (his drawings) were entirely finished while the subject was before him, for he conceives that studies are lessened in value by being retouched in the house"; but a Miss Weeton who knew him well, and was godmother to one of his children, says that "he is employed all summer in taking sketches, and all the winter in finishing them. He is indefatigable: a singular kind of man".

He soon started to gather illustrations for *The Tourist's New Guide to the Lake District,* but as with the Manchester plan, it took much longer than he had hoped, and the final version was not published until 1819. He earned his living with exhibitions of his work, in Ambleside at home and in Keswick, where he rented a room for the purpose; and he also exhibited in Manchester on occasions.

Green was not satisfied with his output, and after completing the Guide Books he intended to publish a series of studies on the neighbourhood of Kendal, centred around the Castle. This was to be followed by one on Preston, featuring the Priory predominantly. Alas, none of this was achieved as by 1820 his health had begun to suffer and, despite his strong constitution, worries and constant exposure to the elements had worn it down. He died on 29th April 1823 and was buried on 3rd May at Grasmere. His wife's words in the Family Bible, to which Roeder had access, held the following lines:-

"My beloved husband died after a lingering illness on 29th April at 18 minutes past 4 o'clock in the morning ... if he would have lived to the 25th August, he would have been 63 years old."

He was survived by four daughters and six sons, as well as his wife. His daughter Jane had been born in the year they settled in Ambleside, 1800, and had been his constant companion; she died at 28 and was buried beside her father and brother William. His wife Anne died on 15th January 1833 and is also buried at Grasmere.

[1]*William Green, the Lakes Artist (1760-1823)*
A Biographical Sketch by Charles Roeder. Reprinted from the Transactions of the Lancashire & Cheshire Antiquarian Society, Vol. XIV.
Published Manchester: Richard Gill, Tib Lane, Cross Street. 1897.

# Chapter 3

# His Family Life

In Miss Weeton's *Journal of a Governess*[1], she writes on 15th September 1810: "I would have introduced you to Mr. Green, who keeps an exhibition of drawings (all his own) in that village where you might have been amused for two or three hours; for he has a great number, two rooms being kept open for the purpose. He draws well, in water colours only. He charges excessively high for them . . . He gets a great deal by showing his landscapes at one shilling each visitor. By that means, and selling drawings now and then, he entirely supports his family, which are very numerous".

William Green was basically a family man. He and Anne had a large family of ten children, who were born between 1799 and 1817. All the children, from the eldest, Elizabeth, down to Thomas Walter, appear in the diary which Green kept, extant for the years 1802-5, 1806-8, 1814-21.

The children were educated by the Reverend Mr. Gritton in Keswick, where their father rented an exhibition room and lodgings. Green, sometimes accompanied by his wife, was often in Keswick on business (he would set off walking from Ambleside, and be picked up by the carrier at Wyburn) and would call to visit his children, and take them out for walks down to Derwentwater.

When the children were older, Green took them out on longer walks, when he was painting or drawing in the hills, and occasionally took one of them on one of his excursions, when he would stay away from Ambleside for a week or more. One September Sarah was his companion on a walk to Coniston, and the following day, when they went to Seathwaite, was "much amused by the appearance of the sea on our scramble to Goat's Water."

The children suffered from the usual ailments, and their remedies. When he was a little boy of 3, Henry was taken very ill one night with croup: bleeding with leeches the following morning "removed the croup, but left a very dangerous inflammation on the lung." Dr. Scambler had given up much hope for his life, but within a few days he was surprisingly recovered. Henry's brother George suffered from croup later in the year. The doctor "bled him in the jugular vein, blistered and purged him with calomel, and lowered his pulse with foxglove", and he was "somewhat better in the morning"! Green also anxiously records bouts of measles, his youngest son Thomas having fits as a baby, and Joshua being troubled with erysipelas, which made for a tiring journey for him back to Keswick. The year before, 1820, Joss had had an accident with gunpowder, which, although his eyes escaped injury, disfigured his face, so that he looked "like an old man of 60."

Green also records what his children have been doing by themselves — the girls visiting Keswick neighbours to drink tea, or going with their brothers on a journey to Kendal, or sometimes dining out, as when they visited Mr. James Fleming at Grasmere. The children were also taken by their father to adult entertainments — to a concert in Kendal, or a hunt in Troutbeck. They attended dances too, under the watchful eye of their father: at Christmas 1819 Mary Anne came with her sister Elizabeth, now married to Mr. Mark Mayson of Portinscale, and Hartley, George and Henry, who all "danced well."

Birthdays did not go unrecorded. His was 25th August. In the diary of 1818 his son Hartley's was 25th May, and was the only entry. Yet his apparent coolness in his diary can be startling. For December 14th 1804 he writes: "finished the three drawings for Mr. Knowlys — Mrs. Green delivered of a dead daughter the child full grown", and on January 23rd 1808 he wrote tersely "My wife was delivered about one in the day of a daughter."

But other entries could be warmer. For instance when he visited Manchester in 1814 he wrote 9th September — an exceedingly pleasant ride all the way from Leicester to Manchester . . . we found my poor mother (actually his step-mother) surprisingly well for a person of 80 — dined at Brother's and drank tea with my mother and Aunt Weston", and on "Sunday, I went to my mother's and walked back with Aunt Evans to my brother's, she walked wonderfully for a person of 82½ — drank tea again at my mother's.

And on April 29th 1804 "had a very pleasant walk with the 3 little chaps round by Rothay Bridge, Miller Steps and home again by the Rydal road" must surely refer to a walk with his young sons. His walks with adults were usually a great deal longer than that.

In a disagreeable episode which remains very obscure, Green in 1803 became involved with a woman called Agnes Brathwaite, on whose "abominable perjuries" he was committed to Kendal jail on 24th August. His confinement was not over-rigorous, as "the worthy jailer Smith" took him out for a walk while he was there; and by 30th August he was back at home in Ambleside, having found Anne and the children as well as he could expect. He was bound in the sum of £40 to appear at the Michaelmas Quarter Sessions in Kendal, the banker Christopher Wilson standing surety for him, for £30. On 7th October Green "went to Kendal where the abominable Agnes Brathwaite forswore herself again, but said the child was born 10th December — before, on the 5th of October". The case was then apparently dropped, and Agnes Brathwaite is not mentioned any more.

One of Green's favourite interests was music, and he records both public concerts and private music-making at home, and when out visiting. The artistic ability of John Harden is rarely remarked on, but Green often enjoyed music in his company. In November 1804 when he dined at Brathay, Green "was much gratified by the musical performances of the worthy couple." In 1807 when he again dined with the Hardens, there was "music by Mr. and Mrs. Harden and Miss Shannon." Then again a month later, there was music "as usual." Sometimes famous musicians came to perform in the Lake District. In April 1805 at Low Wood, Green met the celebrated Mr. and Mrs. Young, who entertained him highly with their singing. In October 1815 a Mr. Scruton came, and stayed for a weekend full of music with the Green family, then went to Kendal to perform in a long concert which Green and his wife attended, together with their daughters Jane and Elizabeth. After lunching with the architect Mr. Webster, the family heard the Messiah in the Parish Church, "the recitative 'Comfort ye' executed by Braham in a very superior state." Afterwards, presumably elsewhere, there was a theatrical performance, including the 'Death of Abercromby', 'Robin Adair', and more music, including a divertimento on the harp, and "a solo concerto on the violoncello." The Greens returned home at half-past one in the morning, but were up to welcome the musicians for breakfast on their way further north; before they left they sang some "excellent glees."

In January 1816 "the new Piano Forte came — an excellent instrument"; the piano tuner came in April, stayed for the night, and accompanied Jane on her violin.

Green was a ready judge of others' musical ability. After dining with the Dixons, he comments that Mrs. Dixon is a respectable piano-player and beautiful singer, and her husband an excellent violinist. After attending Mr. Earl's ball in November 1816 he wrote simply, "Earl a bad fiddler."

There were many other entertainments besides music. Dining out of course figured largely, with such people as the Hardens, and another fellow artist, Julius Caesar Ibbetson, and entertaining friends for dinner at home. There was a card club which met once a week in winter, where Green played with a group of about a dozen, including his doctor, Richard Scambler, and James Fleming of Grasmere and the Partridges, Robert and Edward. Drinking tea as a social activity was also favoured — sometimes with the Wordsworths, at Rydal Mount. Green would go to Low Wood for bowling, and also enjoyed hunting — and it must be remembered that hunting in the Lake District is on foot and not on horseback! He went hunting in Grasmere, and often stayed on for a party in the evening after a hunt. In February 1820, four days after hearing the news of King George III's death, he declined to hunt with his son-in-law, Mark Mayson, "from respect for the memory of the King." In December 1816 Green went to Troutbeck (the southern Troutbeck, not John Peel's) with his sons Joss and Bernard, when they were hunting marts, "it being unlawful to hunt hares when snow was on the ground". In a long account of this hunt, Green refers to himself at one point as being in the "plebeian party." They had dinner at 2.30 of "beef and giblet frye", and an hour later a goose was produced. We know too that Green enjoyed drinking.

Green records when he has had a particularly good meal: after eating at the Swan in Grasmere, with Anne, he writes "the dinner good and cheap, all cheerful . . . " The Royal Oak in Keswick wins special praise — after watching horse-racing at Crow Park Green dined in company there, and had "one of the best ever dinners I have sat down to in the North of England."

And he enjoyed picnics; in the Guide he recounts how one day during a drive up Little Langdale and home by Dungeon Ghyll, "the cloth was laid on the green grass, for that was the table: the cold collation was next produced from the carts, and the writer, though he has been one of many, has seldom witnessed more cheerful gipsyings. The repast being ended, all advanced to the farm called Mill Beck. Those preferring milk to grog or porter were plentifully supplied with it at the house."

There were less fortunate gastronomic experiences: one morning in November 1816 Green was

*Gutterscale.*

*Gutterscale.*

25

*Stones on Loughrigg Fell.*

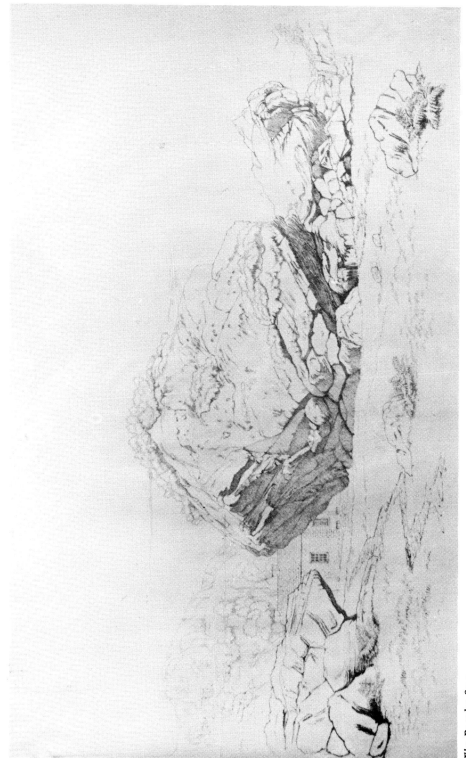

*The Bowder Stone.*

*Bowness.*

*Sprinkling Tarn.*

"extremely unwell by being deprived of my sleep in the night by the illness of my wife, caused as she and I suppose by eating beef stakes for supper."

He was fond of dancing. The first entry in his diary for 1802 is "19th January — Mr. Ibbetson's Dance"; and on 12th May of the same year he danced there again, and did not return home till next day. In 1810 Miss Weeton wrote to her brother: "Mr. Green, the artist, requested me to stand Godmother for his child on Thursday last (11th October). I consented, and spent a most agreeable day. In the evening we had a dance". In 1813 he mentions "our dance, or rather the girls' first dance", and there are many other diary entries showing attendance at Balls at Hawkshead and Ambleside.

(Although she had enjoyed herself, Miss Weeton apparently never wrote a single letter to her god-daughter, though she was a tremendous letter-writer. Here she continues: "A Mr. Lewis, an historic painter from London, come for a few weeks on a jaunt of pleasure, played on the piano for us. Mr. Green has again promised me the pencilled sketches of Dove's Nest. When I get them, I should like to send them to you to copy".)

Green seems to have felt himself an 'off-comer' all his life after moving to Ambleside from Manchester. After drinking with a friend, Mr. Clarkson, in 1803, he declares it was the best time he had had since he came into Westmorland. In September of the following year he made a trip to Furness Abbey to sketch, and recorded, "I was treated in a more kind and liberal manner than I have been by any people in the North of Lancashire and Westmorland, by Mr. Atkinson, his mother and sisters"! In April 1816, musing after John Brownrigg's death, he says he might have thought differently of him had he been born in Ambleside, "the moral code of the people here not being like that of many other places."

One occasionally has a glimpse of Green's neighbours after he has been with them, or heard of their deaths, when he liked to write their obituaries. Mr. Pedder, who had lived at Dove's Nest (near Low Wood, Windermere) "is a very good humoured man and a gentlemanly man when sober, but, nearly tipsy, is peevish and queer".[2] Mr. Gardner, whom he met while staying one Christmas at Chalon Hall near Heversham, is "a good humoured man of great honour and strict integrity". After attending Mrs. Scaler's funeral, Green writes "the mind and the body, to produce good and prevent evil ought constantly to be engaged in such pursuits as are consistent with future prospects of happiness". Occasionally the diary suffers the full force of Green's venom and anger. "Fletcher thy name is quackery", he fumes after being manoeuvred out of renting a house he had had his eye on, by a local headmistress. In April 1820 Green's doctor, Richard Scambler, and his prating wife are "replete with folly", and in writing his obituary a few months later Green "can find very little to praise."

Green was a warm supporter of the monarchy, and wrote a long encomium of George III after hearing of his death in 1820. Two years before, on the King's birthday, he had written, "a venerable and excellent monarch — may his virtues be emulated by succeeding Kings." On July 19th 1821 Green dined at the Salutation Inn at Ambleside, drank the health of the newly-crowned George IV, and sang 'God Save the King' twice.

Green did not go to church every Sunday — sometimes he walked around the house and idled, or went for a walk in the hills; but he notes his attendance at church, in Ambleside, Grasmere or Keswick and the preacher he has heard. William Jackson's sermon at Grasmere was "excellent, and almost free from Westmorland accent!" He heard the same preacher again later, and in 1821 heard Mr. Cocker, "an excellent reader", give a "persuasive sermon of the evangelical kind".

His exhibitions became a regular feature in his life in Ambleside. The diaries are proof of the work involved, for days before he would be discussing the hanging arrangements, the framing and the other arrangements to be made. He trudged the long road to Keswick or often to Wythburn where the carrier, Jackson, would take him to Keswick when the Exhibition was held annually. He also held them in Ambleside and Manchester. To help him he had his 'Exhibitioner' as he called Mr. Robert Watson. On 24th May 1804 he "took a room between the back of the Queen's Head in Keswick of Mr. Brocklebank at a rent of £8 per Annum for an Exhibition room." Three days later he "considered all the morning, got a good dinner and drank a pint of wine." In the next few days he was busy making size, painting signs and colouring the room and "hooking." On 2nd & 3rd June he put up the drawings. Again he made the journey on 4th with the "Miller's cart" to prepare. The joiners were at work on 5th pasting the end of the room. On the 6th & 7th he continued to colour the room, put in the hooks, and part of the tenters, coloured the frames. He was still "hooking", putting in the glasses and titling on 8th and on 10th he had nearly finished the lettering on the sign. At last on 12th he numbered the drawings and wrote the catalogue notes before returning home. Tantalizingly he does not mention how the Exhibition went. But the trouble he took on each occasion was the same. The walls covered with pictures, others on tables, and portfolios of different sizes all round the room, they must have been full shows.

In 1797 he had exhibited two paintings, No. 500 in the catalogue 'Barrow Cascade', and No. 651 'Silver Cove at the head of Enerdale Water', this must of course refer to Ennerdale Water. The Academy lists are full of spelling mistakes; whether they reflect the carelessness of the artists or later wrong transcriptions one cannot tell. In 1798 he exhibited No. 447, 'Derwent Water from Castle Rigg', and in 1801, No. 649, 'View from Kirby Lonsdale Churchyard Westmorland', but this appears to be the last entry, probably because once he had moved to Ambleside he concentrated on his one man shows in the area.

The local families were patrons and indeed reading the diaries one is struck by the continuity of families into this decade. A list includes Pedders, Senhouses, Flemings, Crewdsons, Stanleys, Biglands, Longmires, Wilsons and Stricklands. It could be a list of to-day and he was well-loved by all.

Even after his death Roeder recorded that his Exhibitions were continued by his wife and daughter for some years, when, as Wilson remarks, his etching could be got almost paper-cheap.

Roeder concluded his biographical sketch by quoting a tribute from the French traveller, M. L. Simond, who visited the Lakes in 1811. "Before leaving Windermere, I must mention an artist, who is but little known, Mr. Green, who has resided amongst the mountains, chiefly at Ambleside, during the last ten years. He has studied the details of their forms and physiognomy and renders them in a manner both truthful and original. Moreover his novel method is notable, as the artists have all a conventional and uniform style in regard to the representation of mountains. Those of Mr. Green's are veritable mountains; he says that he knows their anatomy and he is undoubtedly right."[3]

The last word on him as a person may come from Miss Weeton's Journal, again from the letter to her brother written in September 1810. "He (Mr. Green) is a great oddity . . . a man of good size, rather inclining to corpulent, and good, solid, thick legs. His eyes are black and somewhat small, and he does peep so queerly with them! His eyes both look one way, to be sure, but I can seldom catch them looking straight forward. A stranger that was addressed by him would imagine he was talking to someone else; or if no other person was in the room, would stare about him, wondering what the fellow was talking to. Green talks a good deal in an inflated style, and always looks sideways at the object he is speaking to; when he looks directly forward, it is at some piece of furniture or other inanimate object, still talking all the while. I have often much ado to keep my countenance when I hear and see him, though really the man means well; and Oh! he does load one with such great, big, thumping, barefaced compliments; bestowing a pretty decent one on himself now and then."

"Just imagine him standing by the side of you, with his hands crossed before him in a Miss Mollyish style, his intended bow half a courtsey, his fat arms and legs assisting, as in duty bound; his side glances at you every ten seconds, while he softly, sweetly and insinuatingly informs you — that he has made the arts his peculiar study for the last eight years, and that he flatters himself, by his unremitting study he has greatly contributed to their improvement; that he came to Ambleside for that purpose ('tis a great big lie — he came solely to get a living for himself and family, but he is too proud to acknowledge this) and hopes that the time has been employed with equal advantage to the arts and to himself."

"This is his general speech to strangers; the word arts, and artist, he is particularly fond of. His is high and proud to a degree, yet he was originally a drawing master in Manchester, and his wife a player. He certainly draws well — but he needs no trumpeter. He has very great merit in many respects. He is indefatigably industrious, and by his own labour alone in drawing, supports a wife, six children, and two servants, in a respectable style. He is very sober too, and bears a good moral character; and he is laughable, but not contemptible. Mrs. G. is a very respectable kind of woman."

Miss Weeton was a waspish spinster, but the picture is not wholly unkind. It echoes many other tributes to his industry; and it shows that he was indeed a good family man.

---

[1]*Miss Weeton's Journal of a Governess: letters and Journal entries from 1807 to 1837,* found in Wigan and published in 1931: reprinted by David & Charles 1969.

[2]This is borne out by Miss Weeton, who as Governess to Pedder's wife and daughter, shows him to have been eccentric to the point of madness. But as one of her criticisms is that he refused to buy blacking for his family's shoes (and would not spend money on a carriage in order to go to church) and yet spent 10 guineas on a set of etchings from Mr. Green, one can see why Green's comment is not sharper.

[3]*Roeder*, p.31

# Chapter 4

# Green as an Artist

"Man may rise to the contemplation of the Divine through the senses."

Abbot Suger, 12th C.

When William Green settled in Ambleside in 1800, he stepped into the crucible of the new Romantic movement in Britain. It is pertinent to consider the materials from which this crucible was built. From the middle of the 18th century writers and then artists had visited the "Lakes" in a steadily increasing stream and jointly they slowly helped to transform public opinion from one of "Salvatorian" horror, described by the earlier visitors, to a passionate romantic appreciation. By romantic the authors mean, in this context, that the passions of men joined with the beautiful forms and great forces of nature and that men identify with these elements. This transformation did little more than reflect the changing current of aesthetics in Western Europe at this time. Most of the painters who came, except J. Farington, were birds of passage gathering ideas which they could incorporate in their future work, encouraged by the writings of Gray, Gilpin, West and many others. Perhaps some were just following the current fashionable tour. The work of these men, with a very few exceptions such as Turner and Girtin, was not intrinsically important and could be divided into topographical and idealistic landscape. The former were usually made from sites of easy access, often "stations" exactly pointed out by West and other writers. These views were often repetitive and mostly of a "snapshot" simplicity. As for the idealistic school, they might just as well have gone to North Wales or Derbyshire. The opinionated William Gilpin, although a native of Cumberland, was an apostle of this creed and his illustrations of his very successful *Observations on the lakes of Cumberland and Westmoreland* (1780) display a dreary and unidentifiable geological mediocrity. When the topographical artists displayed their work in the south of England they served as most effective tourist publicity. J. Farington published his lithographic *Views of the Lakes* in 1789. These were often used as copies to illustrate the numerous different guide books that were being sold. Indeed there seems to have been little diminution in this publishing bonanza up to the present time. The touring painters, however, showed little sympathy towards the quiet intimacy of the valleys and lakes which became so evident in the literature at the end of the 18th century. Indeed this same criticism is valid for Green's work prior to his settling in Ambleside. For most people it seems that it is necessary to stay long enough to enjoy the bad weather as well as the good, to gain a true appreciation of the countryside. Indeed in his guide Green recommended a stay from the end of June to the end of October. He said too much time was spent at watering places . . . "when frequently the waters do less good than dissipation do (does) injury." But "a summers rambling over rugged ground (of the lakes) would be more beneficial than all the waters in the universe."

There were other more prosaic influences which helped to mould the crucible as well as Green's life. The industrial revolution was creating a new moneyed class, much of it in the North and Midlands. These financially successful people aped the social ways of the old gentry and aristocracy and the Grand Tour was an important pursuit of this class. A year or two in France and Italy was not compatible with the efficient running of the new industries, but two or three weeks in the Lakes, Scotland or North Wales showed the neighbours that one's family had gentle interests. It cost less too. Also, after the Jacobite Wars there had been a gradual but continuing improvement of the main roads in Britain. This, in conjunction with concomitant improvements in stage-coaching, enabled many more citizens to

View from Nr. Ecclerigg

Crummock and Buttermere

Bassenthwaite

Brathay Hall and Langdale Pikes from Low Wood

Friar's Cragg

Grasmere

View of Windermere

Grange in Borrowdale

*William Green.*

embark, with only moderate discomfort, on much longer journeys than had previously been considered. Green must also have been helped by the growing availability of good water colour paints as only towards the end of the 18th century could amateurs easily obtain made up colours. Inspired by the success of the excellent professional watercolourists of that time, many travellers set out for the Lakes with their sketching equipment, mirrors and paints. Green was waiting for them, not only to give them lessons but also to sell them additional colours specially to represent the true Lake District tints.

All these factors were overshadowed by the political unrest in Europe, culminating in the French Revolution and the Napoleonic Wars. Until William Green's death in 1823 there were not many options open to those people who had the leisure to travel even if they could resist the siren songs of the "Lakes" poets.

Let us next consider the psychological and artistic impedimenta that Green brought with him into the crucible. Coming from a lower middle class Manchester family, he understood the need for hard work and this is made very clear in his diaries. He continued to work hard and regularly up to his death not just at the drawing and painting he loved but also at the mechanics of his etching and the presentation of his work to the public. In his diaries he looks forward to future success, but it was his artistic success that he sought before financial security. His Anglican faith was visible rather than assiduous; he apologises in his diaries for his work keeping him from church on Sundays. Politically he was constitutionally blue but emotionally pink, but as his politics required even less observance than his religion there was no real dichotomy in this. He had a clear understanding of his social position in Georgian society and his writings show an undue deference to the gentry. However in matters of art and the aesthetics of nature his opinions bowed to none. Perhaps a little critical of his friends, he was a reasonable man of his time in all respects other than his "passion for his Art".

It is interesting that both Paul Sandby and Green came to painting through mapmaking. Green must surely have seen Sandby's landscape prints and possibly some of his paintings. He certainly used methods of etching and aquatinting that Sandby introduced from the continent. In his Guide (1819) Green admires both Rosa and Claude and states that these men are his artistic guiding stars. It would be very interesting to know if he had seen any of their original works in London. In the late 18th century a quarter of all Claude's work was said to be in the possession of about fifty English Gentlemen; of which Green saw four at Holker Hall. It is surprising, perhaps, that he makes no mention of Gaspard Dughet when so many of that man's works had middle ground lakes with a classical environment. No other sources are mentioned in either the Guide or the diaries. There are two British painters whose work must have influenced him, namely Richard Wilson and Joseph Farington.

In the 1760's when Wilson was asked to paint Welsh landscape, perhaps in response to the Celtic[1] revival, he was faced with the problem of how to paint bare mountains. This was a new idea in painting. In the early 16th century Leonardo da Vinci toured the southern Alps for geological and botanical reasons and sketched the mountains. Again Pieter Breughel in 1552 when travelling from Antwerp to Rome drew the Alps and used these in later paintings. With these exceptions, paintings of mountains *per se* are rare. So Wilson's work of Cader Idris, even if only seen by Green as a print, must have been of seminal interest. Here were mountains without trees or buildings, portrayed without awe. Green would be unlikely to know that the topography was considerably manipulated, but the use of boulders and rocks to build a foreground and the use of a mountain tarn as a middleground became frequent features of his work. Even Wilson's decorative use of humans is later echoed in Green's paintings. Although only using watercolour it appears that Green imitates the technique of painting boulders. Shortly after 'Cader Idris', Wilson painted the 'Great Bridge over the Taaffe'; the etchings made from this were published in 1766. Here the stream with a stony bed, the rocky cliff on the left-hand side of the picture and above all the bridge itself, make the foundations for many of Green's lakeland pack bridges. A further most important point was Wilson's admiration for Claude's "Air". Green also made much of Claude's "Air" and this became a paramount feature in the Ambleside painter's work.

Joseph Farington, a native of Lancashire, spent longer than most artists in the Lakes and returned at later dates to make further drawings. His topographical drawings are most exact and particularly in his sketches of villages and houses some sense of intimacy is achieved, although it is usually in a grand setting. Farington's influence is mostly seen in Green's excellent etchings of buildings throughout the district. It is possible that the two men may have met in London.

This practical middle aged surveyor with a wife and new baby left the relative security of surveying, at which he had already achieved some distinction; turned his back on London and its opportunities; and took his chances as an artist in Ambleside. It would be a hazardous undertaking today even with the benefit of Social Security. In spite of modern climbing gear and boots, present day mountaineering and fell walking in bad weather is still difficult and at times dangerous. In 1800 there were no access roads, no mountain rescue, no way of keeping dry or changing wet clothes until returning home which might take three days. It can be seen from the dates and sites of his drawings that he was an intrepid walker in regions where the only places of rest were shepherds' cottages. Besides having confidence in his artistic and physical abilities, he had a great passion for Nature as she showed herself in the Lake District which not only initiated his venture but maintained it all his life.

If having walk'd with Nature
And offered, as far as frailty would allow,
My heart in daily sacrifice to Truth
I now affirm of Nature and Truth . . .

One impulse from a vernal wood
May teach you more of man,
Of moral evil and of good,
Than all the sages can.

Again Wordsworth in his *Guide to the Lakes* says, whilst referring to a local resident ". . . (He) must have experienced, while looking on the unruffled waters (of a lake) that the imagination is carried into the recesses of feeling otherwise impenetrable". It would be almost inconceivable with his passion, that Green would not have been powerfully influenced by Wordsworth and, as will be shown later, in turn, reciprocated this effect. It must be borne in mind that when the painter settled in the square at Ambleside, his house was very near to Wordsworth's stamp office. Green painted those faces of nature of which Wordsworth wrote in his early years, albeit more a fern and burdock man than one of celandine and daffodil.

These then are some of the elements of Green's amalgam. Principally in this chapter it is his watercolours that are discussed. These fall roughly into two categories. He had to make a living and to do this, in common

*Langdales.*

*Ullswater.*

with many other painters, he painted 'postcards', which were numerous, repetitive, and dull. These are excluded from this analysis. From the first two years in Ambleside have survived some good small wash drawings of scenes throughout the district. These, referred to in his diary, may just have been to illustrate special copies of other authors' guide books. Certainly this method of drawing has not been seen at a later date, and it would have been difficult to produce this quality and style of work in quantity. In 1804 he produced his first popular set of aquatints, *Sixty Views of the Lakes*. That they were popular can be shown by the water marks on the prints, some of which were reprinted repeatedly for 20 years. Some of the early prints were given additional colour by the artist and his friends. Little of his work of the next three years is known, but from that time until 1814 he produced much of his best drawing in pencil and watercolours. His system seems to have evolved by 1807, whereby he made pencil drawings of exceptional quality, sometimes with marginal notes on colours, light, sun position, and any licence he may have taken with the topography. These drawings were always made between the last few days of August and the end of October. He seems to have largely ceased to make these large sketches by 1814 although smaller and less interesting ones exist until 1820. Many of his best watercolours have been made from these splendid sketches, but for the most part the paintings are not dated. During this period from 1807 to 1814 William Green also produced his best etchings, although some later aquatints were very good.

From his diaries it would appear that he was interested in trying his hand at oil-painting. In October 1814 he writes "What would be ... so interesting as a series of fine oil paintings describing this beautiful scenery". This was in relation to a proposed exhibition in Manchester. Although there are at least ten references to his actually painting in oils in his diary, there are no comments on the medium in the guide. Unfortunately the authors do not know of any existing Green oil painting.

Although William Green was deprecatory about his own writing it is most happy for us that his Guide (1819) sets out clearly the aspirations of his art. This knowledge is expanded by the more personal comments of his diary. Unfortunately his paintings passed from fashion and the public eye and much has been lost and awaits discovery. From his diaries it is evident that the sheer mass of work he achieved was remarkable. Scarcely a day passed in his diary at the peak of his creative period without some reference to his work. It is not possible to assess his total output as no serious work has been undertaken on him till now. Roeder tentatively puts it at 1000 finished pictures and complains that there were few at the British Museum, still fewer in provincial libraries. The constant flow of visitors to his annual exhibitions in Ambleside and Keswick must have been responsible for carrying his work all over the country. He also exhibited in Ulverston and in his diaries talks of preparations for big shows in Manchester and Liverpool, but it is not known if these took place. Hartley Coleridge's comment has been mentioned in an earlier chapter, and it emphasises his industry. Part of this employment was walking over mountains and fells seeking sites for making his drawings or pursuing his botanic and geological interests. He engaged Jonathan Otley[2] to do the scientific work necessary for his guide books, and John Gough[3] made the botanical notes required. Otley was mentioned in the diary of 17th September 1816, when he joined Green at Ennerdale for the evening and next morning "Finished the tops of the mountains" is all he says of his work. On 1st March 1818 "Mr. Otley and I walked to a little beyond Barrow Beck — very windy, the spray ran upon the water, but no pillars of vapour". Green displayed more than most writers his total capacity for visual appreciation. He was totally involved with looking, both at the fine details of the minutest forms and tiny plants and of the scene as a whole. His words in their very profusion are his earnest attempt to convey to the reader with almost desperate intensity the deep pleasure he drew from what he observed. His reactions caused him pleasure, fury, deep repose or inner peace. He strove with words as he strove with brush, pen, or etching needle to give the public equal sensations.

Weather often affects the way artists work. When Constable came to the Lake District, the rain, wind and constant clouds disturbed him. Although he made some magnificent paintings and drawings of it he preferred a milder climate to produce his masterpieces. William Green was fascinated by the ever changing effects which caused the Cumbrian weather. He took an interest in it from a scientific point of view and his etchings and aquatints show he had a clear understanding of different types of cloud formation and their associated weather. Many entries in his diaries describe dramatic storms over the mountains when he was out making sketches. On 20th February 1803 he recorded a visit to Wastwater, which he reached over Langdale Head, "Went down to the foot of the water, got up the side of the skrees, where there was the most awful and tremendous storm of thunder and lightning and hail I ever remembered. I got wet thro' and was kindly and hospitably treated at Mrs. Fletcher's sisters ..." Despite the weather, Green continued to go out of doors to paint and draw. He caught the atmosphere of those grey days when the clouds hang low on the hills and the colours

*Stockley Bridge.*

are sombre. He made the most of the clear patches of brilliant blue sky fleetingly appearing through the white storm clouds. He excelled when he caught fine rays of sunlight dappling the surface of a lake. He handled superbly and with deep understanding, that basic interrelation of landscape and its prevailing climatic conditions. Many artists would only wish to portray Windermere in sunny weather and would turn it into a different place, but he managed to evoke any real day in the Lake District as it were in its right clothes.

Though one cannot claim for Green the sublimity of Turner, the clarity of Cotman or the magnificence of Constable, he was one of the most faithful topographical artists to paint the Lake District. Added to his faithful representation was his own flavour of the area which no one else has been able to maintain over such a long period. Green's mountains are and were for him unlike those of Scotland with their purple grandeur and exotic shapes, nor did they have their awesome desolation. The lofty Alps of Victorian blue with their Annecy lakes were remote from his countryside. Both these errors were often made before and after Green. Very few found the unique blue-green colour of the lakeland hills. In Wordsworth's Guide, when writing of lakes, he stresses that "grandeur as connected with magnitude, has seduced persons of taste into a general mistake on this subject". This he applies also to mountains, holding the combination of small hills with varied textures are more beautiful than grand magnitude. As a general rule Green in his Guide recommends the skies be a quarter blue and three quarters grey, and he holds himself to this idea most strictly. These large strong skies create an intimacy in the landscape which is an essential lakeland characteristic. His gods lived in the lakes, hills and clouds among which he walked, not in a high cerulean Italian sky.

On the endboards of his Guide, he states "the drawings profess to represent those grand and beautiful effects which are produced by the action of the sun, as interrupted and modified by air, clouds and vapour, upon the varied surfaces of a mountainous country." In the preface of his book of etchings 78 Studies (1809) he says "He has always considered fidelity of imitation is the first improvement in the fine arts." Nearly all his work follows this dictum, and that which does not is annotated accordingly. There is one large interesting watercolour with a background of the Langdales, a middle ground of Hornby Castle and a foreground of the lower falls at Rydal; all this is explained at the foot

46

*Brother Water.*

of the picture. Alas, like many of his watercolours this one has faded and discoloured, the blue pigment being the most faded. Again his drawing of Goody Bridge, Grasmere, (Small Prints, 1814) has a footnote saying "To improve the composition the stepping stones have been brought nearer the houses than they actually are."

The word 'picturesque' appears several times in the Guide. W. Gilpin, the self appointed arbiter of taste, defined this word as "that which would look well in a picture". Such a word may be useful to a literary man but it throws little light on Green's intentions except when he uses it in a negative sense; in one chapter he states a subject was "unpicturesque and consequently not worth an artists attention". So rather than use this overworked word a more precise description of the artist's style and concepts will be attempted with the help of his own text. Green criticised previous guides, correctly, for their geographic vagueness and their lack of adventure in seldom stirring from the main roads and 'stations' as the viewpoints were called. Gilpin and Budworth should perhaps be excluded from this censure; certainly Mrs. Radcliffe's description of her coach ride to the top of Skiddaw (appendix of West's Guide) exonerates her. He believed "a moderate degree of elevation relieves all objects on an horizontal plane from that huddled confusion resulting from a lowly point of view". As the lakes in the district are usually linear this technique was most useful in foreshortening a long lake and so forming a more round midground subject. Gray had stated that the painter's view of a landscape had always to be from a low point. Green insisted the artist had always to scramble a bit to get an ideal vantage position. Whilst discussing Derwentwater he discourages drawing from a boat or small island, "the passion for boat prospects is owing to the delusive fascinations of the water." "High or low will seldom suit the taste of a painter who will always move over the surface of his near grounds till the component parts of his subject appear to him to be arranged in the best possible order." This selection of an elevated vantage point, which often required much exertion to reach, is an approach which separated Green from many of the earlier painters, but was subsequently followed by many. In the Guide and Small Prints, (1814), he is very specific about the exact spot from which a particular scene should be drawn. Unfortunately he applied the same stricture to himself and some of his works are rather limited. The same view exactly appears in his whole range of media. This does however help in identification of some of his paintings. His was the first Guide to specify the names of each fell, beck, and tarn visible from his view point.

Although he gives Rosa and Claude as his mentors, he seldom followed their rigid classical composition, indeed in his mountainous terrain this would have been very difficult. However most of his paintings have a classical fore, middle and back ground. There are imposed on this construction many lessons that seem to come from Richard Wilson. Earlier in his life he had problems with the long thin lakes forming a strong dividing and horizontal midground; this gave an unhappy prominence to the foreground. In his foregrounds he liked "trees, which with a little scholastic management, will exhibit on paper many rare assemblages". "Rocks, though sturdy materials, are often more accomodating than trees for there are many scenes known to the writer which are profuse in such accomodation." The Guide quotes Gilpin, not one of Green's favourite authors, as rejecting the general view in favour of the small particular detail. "But he who is in quest of picturesque scenery of the Lake (Derwent) must travel along the rough side screens that adorn it and catch its beauties as they arise in smaller portions, its little bays, and winding shores . . . its deep recesses, and hanging promontories, its garnished rocks and distant mountains." Although Green took heed of this advice and made such the subjects of many successful paintings, his main strength was in his large scale landscapes. During the discussion on foregrounds, he frequently comments on how the appearance of an area could be improved by thoughtful planting. His pen lashed friend and foe alike. Miss Pritchard of Croft Lodge at Clappersgate, where he was a frequent visitor, was set out in the book as having lands too thick with trees. His host of many a good evening, Mr. Harden, at Brathay Hall, was set up as an example of one who did not plant enough trees. At Derwentwater "Beyond Barrow Beck, is presented a scene of desolation, almost sufficient to draw tears from the eyes of the traveller of feeling, who would certainly lose nothing if he were conducted through it blindfold . . ." "The deformity of the Manesty side, is now held forth to public view, over the miserable patch of near-ground bordering the lake." He was so distraught by the "vernal desolation of avarice" after 1809 at Lodore and Manesty that "dreading farther mischief," he made drawings of the lake margin from Stable Hills to Isthmus. Again referring to Derwentwater he laments nature "despoiled of its charms by sordid insensibility and all its leafy honours laid low". He preferred native trees but accepted some "exotic foreigners" although larches, referred to as "spike heads", he did not like. It is interesting that in Wordsworth's copy of 60 Large Prints the poet has corrected the title of a tree which Green has misnamed. Would that today we had outspoken men of the calibre of Wordsworth and Green to save the landscape from rape and pillage.

But to return to the composition of foregrounds, there are not instructions about man and animals. This perhaps reflects the painter's preoccupation with nature seen through the eyes of a romantic. In most of the paintings the foreground is decorated with humans or domestic animals or both. His humans looked rather like classical statues and the sheep and cows like hairy rocks. He was fully aware of this limitation and it is likely that he got assistance from Lishman and Richardson with this aspect of his work. In September 1814 he declared in his diary that when he became rich he would hire figure painters. "As soon as I am rich I mean to engage some of the very finest artists in their respective lines to paint figures into the landscapes, but these must be of a large size, and if executed in a superior manner will find many admirers". At best, his figures are ornaments set against the splendours of Nature. However large and good his bought figures may have been, they could only have detracted from his landscapes. Buildings, also, seldom appear in his paintings but this was not because he lacked the ability as his etchings show. Bridges, on the other hand, were included on every occasion that could be contrived and were a common topic in his etchings. In general his foregrounds were not very successful and indeed often seem an irrelevant hangover from his classical training.

"Every professional man knows, (at least he ought to know) that . . . a scene with the sun immediately behind him wants air, a quality generally considered as absolutely necessary . . . on the other hand if the sun is within his vision, it probably has too much. Claud Lorrain sometimes painted that celestial luminary in his pictures, but, if not, the sun was but little out of it — a choice generally to be preferred to all others." In this context 'air' means the varying amounts of water as vapour or small droplets that were held suspended in the atmosphere. This could occasionally, in Green's case, be augmented by smoke from the many charcoal burners who worked in the lakeland woods. The 'air' was an extension of both the lakes and clouds. Green sets out the climatic conditions which give rise to the different degrees of 'air'. So hot sun, after much rain (not an uncommon feature of the Lakes, he assures us) when unaccompanied by wind produces "a medium which is the cause of that wonderful diversity of appearances especially in a mountainous country." Too much sun, however, gives rise to

48

*Lodore Falls.*

"a redundant and unsightly vapour". Many hot and calm days produce a rarefied atmosphere which though "fine for distant, is a temporary ruin to the beauty of near objects." Heavy rain succeeded by dry and sunless weather are good for near objects "but there will be little beauty in the distances." Ideally the components of the shadowed side of objects at five miles should be "just not invisible." He warns that there is not uncommonly a great deal of rain after midsummer, between the hay and corn harvests, which diminishes the likelihood of satisfactory 'air'; the hardy traveller will be recompensed by flitting clouds, mists and roaring waterfalls. Both Wordsworth and Green blame West (Guide 1778) for encouraging visitors in July and August which are almost always the wettest months. There is no particular season that gives the best 'air', but although there may be more "heavenly blue" in June he observed some of the finest atmosphere in September and October. As when he talks about colour, he distinguishes between the painter's requirements and those of the sightseer; so a dry heat may produce an aerial density in the atmosphere very favourable to view the scenery, which if lit by "a cloudless sky will be too general to please the (painter's) eye of taste." So much for his friend J. C. Ibbetson's sunlit views of Ullswater and Windermere. "The face of nature under one broad and universal glare (a cloudless midsummer day) is not propitious to the feelings of an anxious spectator; but this monotony can only be of short duration, because the declining sun... produces shadows; these gradually expanding, uniting and finally on the setting of the sun.. exhibit an almost infinite variety of form, of tone and of colour." Again whilst saying the sun has charm at dawn, and is fine at noon, it is "often better at about three and is ... frequently exquisitely beautiful on the approach of evening."

However the significance of the air was not simply its varying degrees of opacity; the colour produced by the light on the water particles was vital. "Now the colours of which the air is composed are blue, red, and yellow and an infinite variety of tint is derived from their mixture." "The air is never of one self-colour only, but is often of two colours, with a little of the third." He continues, "Of all atmospheres those inclining to the yellow and the green are the most unhappy; and the most grateful to the feelings those of a grey somewhat inclined to purple; but a reddish purple hue is not only unpleasant in nature, but ought to be studiously avoided in a picture." It would be interesting to know if Green's ideas about colour in the 'air' were original in view of the developments in the analysis of air colour by painters later in the nineteenth century. He himself never used his pigments in other than a most orthodox manner.

For his own pictures he preferred the early autumnal colours. Although he extols the yellow of spring, the green of summer, and "the changling dresses of autumnal tints"; these were for the sightseers not the painter. Spring was too yellow for the purposes of painting, and he agreed with Wordsworth that the greens of summer were monotonous. "The burning tints that immediately precede the falling of the leaf should be avoided. The happy medium mean between the extremes of hot and cold furnishes to the chaste and sober eye all that can be wished for." The most beautiful colour was "celestial azure", but it must not be overdone. At this point it is interesting to note that a number of Wordsworth's opinions on colour and air of the lakeland landscape are very similar to Green's. Wordsworth did not comment much on these matters in the first edition of his Guide but they are clearly set out in the second edition (1820). That was two years after Green published his Guide in which he sets out these quoted ideas. So it may be that Green influenced the way that the great poet looked at his surroundings; certainly in the later editions of Wordsworth's Guide he acknowledges the value of the painter's book.

It can be seen in this chapter that Green has given clear directions from where the picture should be painted. The cloud cover as well as the atmospheric conditions are precisely defined. He suggested the time of day and the season of the year when a painter of taste would be most satisfied by the sun's position, the colours and the shadows. To his credit he used these dicta only as the basic stepping stones of his own work: the tools but not the finished product. His talents may not have been great but his importance lies in his using them all to express in painting his romantic vision. This sense of oneness with nature is displayed by the manner in which he combines the lakes, the mountains and the sky, and fuses them with his 'air'.

It is water, as lakes, tarns or rivers, which is used to give a bright setting for the mountains, often distracting the attention from the, perhaps, less satisfactory classical neargrounds. The lakes, or water, are seldom still and blue, reflecting mirror images of the detailed hills. They adopt in a lively fashion the colours and shadows of the sky and the surrounding fells, on their rippling surfaces. Sometimes mists may lie on the surface of the water and stretch up towards the clouds. Frequently the water is decorated with boats as well as islands. The painter has given us most interesting information of the types and uses of craft on the different lakes, but this is of secondary importance to his using the water as a well-lit stage to the main theme, the mountains.

The mountains, that he knew and loved so well, are portrayed with great feeling for their surface texture as well as their individual shapes. Indeed it would be possible to identify some fells from the attention he gives to the geology and his affection for each fold of rock and each rattling, winding ghyll, without seeing the characteristic outline of the peak. Although this may seem to be of more interest to a mountaineer it does give a most convincing sense of reality to his hills and this without a sterile exactitude. The site from which the mountains were drawn would be chosen so the different peaks arranged themselves to their best advantage whilst retaining their correct topographical position. Probably no other mountains in Britain have such extensive scope for a natural arrangement of marvellously assorted shapes in breadth as well as depth. Green painted them with the greatest of understanding and sensitivity. As has been previously noted he gave much attention to the unique colour of the Cumbrian mountains and this he combined with the sunlight and shadows falling on the hills so skilfully that it is possible for an observer with local knowledge, to tell the warmth of the sun or the time of day. Just as the mountains give colour to the lakes, so in turn do they reflect the colours of the sky.

Green had a good knowledge of weather and cloud formation, and with his regulation patch of "celestial azure" his skies were carefully painted. It is possible to see in some of his work that rain is imminent as a warm front spreads into the landscape from the Irish Sea. In others the high cumulus is breaking up to give a lovely summer evening. In common with many northern European painters his strong, bright but cloudy skies concentrate attention on the land below: his gods inhabited the rugged countryside not blue Mediterranean heavens. As the lake mists rise up to the hills so the clouds trail down the mountains and valleys to embrace the earth. This might seem artificial to those who have not had the joy of standing on the fells and watching this happen. The colour of the sky permeates the mountains and is reflected by the lakes which also took on the mountain colours. These confluent tones helped to fuse and unite his landscapes.

But if the water is the floor, the hills the walls and the sky the ceiling, it is the 'air' that quickens the scene. The mists, the haze, the rain, the sunbeams (one can almost see the wind at times) fill the stage and create the ecstatic sense of unity essential for a romantic painter. When he concentrated his abilities on the grand and beautiful aspects of the Cumbrian landscape, William Green was a marvellous romantic painter.

"I realised that our existence is nothing but a succession of moments perceived through the senses."

J. J. Rousseau, 1765.

[1]Dunmail, last King of Cumberland, was killed and his sons blinded for confederating with King Leolin of Wales around 944 A.D.

[2]Otley was born in 1766 near Loughrigg Tarn and went to Keswick making a living by basketry but he learnt to repair clocks which he did for forty years. He studied natural sciences and acted as a guide, as did Hutton and Graves and lived to the age of 91, after publishing a map in 1818 which corrected many of the mistakes of previous maps. He invented an ingenious compass which he placed on top of his walking stick and carried a barometer with which he calculated the height of the hills.

[3]John Gough was born in Kendal in 1757 and went blind as a result of small-pox but, despite this, became a leading botanist, philosopher and mathematician. He died in 1825, highly reputed. His essays had been published in *Journals of the Manchester Philosophical Society*, and also in *Nicholson's Journals*. In Kendal Museum there is an interesting case beneath his bust illustrating his work.

# Chapter 5

# A Study of his Printing and Etching by Donald Wilkinson

William Green's first prints date from 1796: these were, *A Series of Picturesque Views of the North of England, drawn from nature and engraved by Wm. Green, consisting of forty-eight views of the Lakes* and priced at £12.12s.6d. They were published by Green himself at 3 Windmill Street, Manchester on the 19th January 1796.

They are large aquatints delicately hand-coloured, and, in the ones that I have seen, the aquatint is very grey and even, quite unlike the later colour aquatints of 1815. The size of the prints is 21½″ x 16½″.

I was first introduced to his etchings in the very printing studios in London to which Green sent many of his plates to be editioned. I was having some of my aquatint plates of the Lake District steel-faced and when, in conversation with Mr. McQueen, he discovered that I came from this area, he recalled that in the past his forebears had printed for another artist from the Lakes. I was intrigued by this and so he went to the store room and eventually returned with a pile of prints. These turned out to be prints of William Green's soft-ground etchings taken as proofs from the plates in the early 1800's.

I was also shown an entry in an old ledger of the period to the effect that plates sent by "Wm. Green of Ambleside" by waggon were ready for collection at a particular address in London.

When one reads Green's journals there are various entries which refer to "McQueen", and to the preparation of proofs and the parcelling of plates for dispatch to London for printing.

"31st Nov. Wrote letters and sent box off to Manchester on the way to Mr. McQueen in London."

Sometimes things went wrong.

"2nd Oct... I heard the boxes were arrived from London, and on the 4th sorted the ten guinea etchings but found in a most unaccountable (sic) that all 13 Conistons with about as many more were pricked through with nails..."

One of the points that distinguishes Green from many of the artists who made prints of the Lake District at this period was the fact that he was one of the few who prepared and drew on the plates and etched the images himself. Other artists making prints of the Lake District who did this were William Westall and Fielding. Most of the Lake District prints at this time were made by craftsmen from either paintings or drawings or developed from sketchbook studies produced by painters who never actually touched the print themselves.

The original painting was interpreted by the technician into marks that were possible in etching or aquatint; this gives most of these prints a stiff, airless quality.

When one sees an aquatint or a soft-ground etching by William Green alongside one of these prints, one is immediately aware of the difference. There is a feeling of light in the best of Green's work and a directness and freshness in the use of aquatint and of line.

Another difference was the fact that Green lived in the Lake District rather than just visiting or touring through it. He would see the landscape in all its moods throughout the year, walking on the fells and round the lakes, walking between Ambleside and Keswick to his exhibition rooms there. This awareness is evident in the best prints, in the feeling of light on the breast of a fell or a break in the cloud in one of his small aquatints. One gets a sense of the scale of the landscape, it remains the Lakes and never becomes the Alps.

Another set of prints was published in 1804. These were again aquatints and some of the prints were finished in watercolour.

*Ullswater from Martindale.*

*Blea Tarn.*

*Raven Crag.*

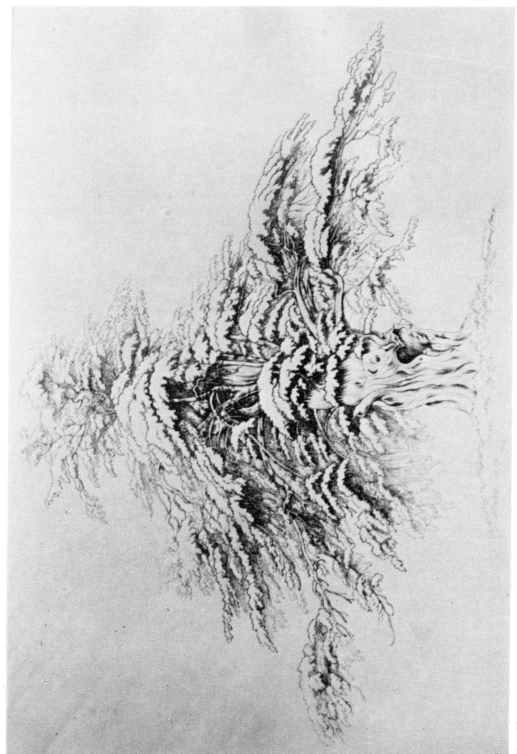

*Yew Tree.*

*Birch trees in Coombe Gill.*

*Rydal Park.*

*Dove Crag in Hartshope.*

Aquatint is a process of achieving tone instead of line by etching a metal plate: the metal used by Green would be copper, and this would then be covered with resin dust. The white areas of the design are stopped-out with varnish before the plate comes into contact with the acid. The particles of resin act as an acid resist, the acid attacks the plate between the resin granules producing minute irregular dots bitten into the plate, the tone of which can be controlled by the length of time the plate is allowed to remain in the acid. It is possible to build up a design through various tones by repeated immersions in the acid and stopping-out with varnish. One can also use a variety of fine or coarse resin grounds. In many of the Green aquatints the foreground is achieved by using a much coarser resin than in the distant hills and sky.

When the etching process is completed the resin and varnish are removed by using a solvent and the plate is cleaned and polished. The plate is now ready for taking a first print, that is, for proofing. The plate is placed on a hot plate and the printing ink is forced into the marks bitten by the acid into the surface of the metal, the ink is cleaned, wiped off the areas where no marks have been etched by using pads of muslin. It is a slow process and must not be hurried. The objective is to clear the surface without removing ink from the bitten areas. Wiping an aquatint is one of the more difficult procedures.

When this process is completed, the plate is ready for printing and is placed on the bed of the etching press. Paper which has previously been dampened is placed on top of the plate and then felt blankets over all, the whole is rolled through the press between the heavy rollers. The blankets are folded back and the printing paper slowly lifted from the plate. One now has a print which is a reversed image of the drawing. This gives one an idea how the print, that is the working on the plate, is progressing and if there are any offending areas or marks these can be removed from the plate by scraping and burnishing the metal. The plate can then be reworked in these areas or in fact the whole can be taken a stage further by laying another ground of resin and immersing in the acid again. Another proof is taken and so the print is built up over a period of time.

There are various entries in Green's diaries setting himself a timetable for the completion of series of plates for his publications:-

" 8 Sunday settled this book and wrote letter — 24 plates done with the first ground in 32 days — I think when the days get long — one of these plates may be done in a day...
9 Finished Wast Water and Lowswater & laid Grounds onto Plates.
10 Prepared Hawes Water — Coniston — Wallow barrow Crag.
11 Finished 2 Conistons.
12 Finished Wallow barrow & Hawes water so that the thirty plates were got through in 36 days or 5 weeks.
13 Burnished.
14 Burnished.
15 Sunday. Will it be possible to finish the 12 — 2 guinea plates the 2nd thirty small ones and the thirty of which the first ground has been done by the first of April next — or the end of March — give opinion on this...?"

It often takes various stages of etching, proofing and burnishing before a satisfactorily completed plate is ready for final printing and editioning.

In these early aquatints by Green the skies are produced by various bitings and stopping-out of the aquatint, the varnish has been applied with a small brush. There is no evidence of an outline on the contour of fell and sky; the whole plate has been achieved by the careful organisation of tonal variation.

In 1808 *Green's Sketches of Scenery of the English Lake District,* was published on June 24th. This is a large landscape portfolio of soft-ground etchings.

It was thought that Green took his large prepared copper plates out into the landscape and worked on them in front of the actual view, but when one looks at a print of a recognisable location the image is not reversed as would have been the case if a direct drawing onto the plate had been made from nature. In fact there are various references in his diaries to his taking his etching equipment out into the landscape — but whether this was soft-ground plates is not made clear.

"Oct. 7th. Etched the Bridge House from the Beck — Mr. Harden & two clergymen came into the beck to see me — they preached & read prayers on the Sunday."
"Oct. 9th. Carted all my engraving apparatus to Rydal Mount & when there made two drawings of the Mount..."
"5th Nov. Etched from Mr. Partridges field..."

*Wastwater.*

Some of his soft-ground plates of plants — tree roots and details of vegetation and rocks could have been drawn on the spot, in fact where the reversal of the image was not of importance or obvious.

The way he carried out most of his large soft-ground etching was to make drawings on the spot on very thin paper the actual size the final print was to be. A number of these drawings still exist.

On returning to his studio the drawing was turned over and he would go over the marks of the original drawing visible through the paper. The copper plate was prepared with a covering of wax-ground, which remained soft to the touch. The reversed drawing was laid on top of the soft-grounded plate and pressure was applied with a pencil over the marks of the drawing. When the paper was removed it lifted up the wax-ground where the pencil had been and exposed the metal. The exposed areas of the plate could then be etched in a weak acid solution, care being taken not to bite through the wax-ground. This method can give all the nuances of a pencil drawing.

In a number of his soft-ground etchings one can discern the actual texture of the paper the original drawing was made on, which has been transferred to the plate by the pressure of the pencil in the larger tonal areas.

The particular portfolio I saw had twenty-seven etchings many being straight-forward views of Ambleside and elsewhere but included were prints of 'Oak trees in Rydal Park', of 'Yew tree in Patterdale churchyard' and 'Birch trees in Coom Gill'. These images show best William Green's ability to handle a large-scale image. These are 30″ x 21″ and are much less about recording a particular view and more about trying to come to terms with the atmosphere and structure of the place.

Various groups of soft-ground etchings were published between 1808 and 1810.

In 1815 Green published *A series of 60 beautifully coloured plates of the Lakes of Lancashire, Cumberland & Westmorland,* priced at £5.5s. and dated 1st June.

These were aquatints and are some of the most beautiful and inventive prints that Green produced. In these prints a combination of two and sometimes three colours has been used on the one plate. The foreground is usually a relatively coarse aquatint and is printed in umber; a more delicate aquatint is used for the distance and sky and printed in prussian blue. Where the two colours meet there is often a soft misty violet which gives the image a feeling of air and space.

In many of the prints one gets a sense of the particular light and weather and the effect of these on the fells. He has captured the characteristic light of the hill country.

If one looks beyond the picturesque formula for the foregrounds of figures, animals or rocks to the hills, lakes or sky, the prints have a delicacy and personality all of their own.

Why these particular prints stand out in my opinion from so many produced for the tourists of the time, is because the artist has not just reproduced his drawings on to plates but he has been able to produce marks that are alive and work within the context of the print. The colour although simple does give a feeling of the atmosphere and time of year. Some of the prints have a quality of Chinese painting in their suggestion of descending cloud and of mist in front of mountains.

I have seen a number where three colours are used: a burnt umber and prussian blue with an introduction of terre verte in trees and foliage. In others a burnt sienna appears in rocks. 'Langdale Head from Wallend,' is an impressive little print: as well as aquatint it appears to have soft-ground etching on the fell and rocks. In the print of 'Raven Crag on Leathes water,' there is a feeling of space and atmosphere.

There are various publications of etchings after this date — many of buildings and views around Keswick and Ambleside — but although the drawing is more accomplished they do not, for me, have the poetry or imagination of the aquatints of 1815.

*Ullswater.*

# Chapter 6

# Relations with other Artists

In the early years of the nineteenth century, life must have been fairly pleasant in the Lake District. Not only Green's diaries but those of the Fleming family and of the artist at Brathay Hall, John Harden, were full of the social events, musical evenings, long rides, walks, dances, dinner parties and drinks or meals at local inns. The artists in the area seem to have seen much of each other.

Although she understood J. C. Ibbetson well, Rotha Mary Clay did not make any reference to Green in her book on Ibbetson. Yet there are six references to meetings with the Julius Ibbetsons in the early diaries, 1801-4. On visiting Hawes Water in 1801 for the first time, Wm. Green in a note to the celebrated Mr. Julius Ibbetson, described Hawes Water as "Borrowdale, with a lake in it." Earlier in the same season, he and Mr. Ibbetson had studied together in Borrowdale. In 1802 he records "19th January — Mr. Ibbetson's dance" and then a few days later he dined at Mr. Ibbetson's. On 13th March he "went to Mr. Ibbetsons" and in April "Mr. Ibbetson and family are dining." On 12th May Mr. Ibbetson held another dance and William Green stayed the night. He also went sketching with J. C. Ibbetson. On 20th September they set off to Pooley Bridge, referred to as "Pawley" Bridge, drawing Brother's Water and "Ulles Water" on the way — "slept at Mardale after drawing Ulles and Hawes." On February 23rd 1804 "left Ambleside with the Fieldings and Ibbetson — took a room between the back of Queen's Head in Keswick at a rent of £8 per annum for an exhibition room; returned and at Wyburn found Mr. & Mrs. Grasmere Ibbetson — drank tea and were very merry." This must have referred to Mr. & Mrs. J. C. Ibbetson junior. On February 27th 1813, "Persons to be written to..." included Julius Ibbetson junior. Julius Ibbetson senior died in 1817 and although there is no mention of the Ibbetsons in between 1813-21, the families must have still been in touch, although J. C. Ibbetson senior had moved to Yorkshire and he is buried at Masham. In 1821 on 10th June, "Mr., Miss and Master Ibbetson called at noon — I was very glad to see Mrs. Ibbetson."

The Hardens were also frequent visitors. The first diary entry was on 26th February 1804 when Green spent the evening with "Mr. and Mrs. Wilcocks and Mr. Harddon," (his spelling of people's names often varies). On 24th November of the same year he "exhibited to Mr. Lloyd and Mrs Southey — and saw Mr. Harden — went to see Mrs. Sharpe and the poor Lady." 27th, "Finished Wastwater and dined with Mr. and Mistress Harden, was much gratified by the musical performances of the worthy couple and their drawings".

If that sounds a rather patronizing remark one can certainly detect real admiration in a later entry, which has been noted in Chapter 2, "afternoon dined with Mr. and Mrs. Harden, musicly Mr. & Mrs. Harden and Mrs. Shannon exquisite pianoforte by both ladies — Mrs. Harden in the upper octave quite excellent", (16 Feb. 1807). In 1816 in November his next mention "... Mr. Harden came and a comfortable party of faces" was his descriptive if rather enigmatic remark. On 7th October 1816 there is the last reference to Harden — "Etched the Bridge House from the Beck. Mr. Harden and two clergymen came into the beck to see me — they preached and read prayers on the Sunday".

On his visits to London he went to see Pyne and Reinagle but the entries are not very illuminating on either artist. 30th March 1808 "saw a woman on Blackfriar's Bridge who had just been killed by a horse which had run away — the horse was stopped just about half way between that market and the bridge, drank tea and supped with Mr. Hills — Mr. Pyne was there — met Mr. Reinagle". He also mentions writing to Pyne on another occasion. Another print maker of the time, Bellers, referred to by Green sometimes as "Beller" was working in the area at the time. On 17th August 1813 "walked to Bowness to assist Mr. Bellersis with his views". 21st, "Mr. Bellasis came washed his subjects". He must have then done some painting on Mr. Bellersis' work as there are two more references to his colouring and finishing the colouring for Mr. Bellersis[1]. Also, when in London he used to visit his

*Rydal Mount.*

former teacher John Landseer and also mentioned going with him to see plates, "and compositor printer at work". Landseer praised his *Seventy-eight Studies from Nature* 1808-1810 and talked about it in some detail in the *New London Review* of 1810.

He did not mention meeting Constable when the latter came up to stay at Brathay in 1806, where he stayed with the Hardens. Although he did know George Gardner, who was born on 19th September 1778, he did not mention meeting his father Daniel Gardner, the portrait painter who was born in 1750 and died in 1805. Although he was certainly closely 'in' with the artistic and literary circle so often described in John Harden's diaries he was not entirely accepted in the more intimate social sense. The only time John Harden refers to Green in his diary was in 1802 — "From Ambleside we took our road to Rydal first having visited Mr. Green's Exhibition of his drawings amongst which indeed I saw some clever ones and felt an inclination to purchase but did not."[2]

Southey, Wordsworth, Quillinan, Hartley Coleridge, De Quincey, Arnold and John Dalton are all frequently mentioned in the diaries. He also knew the well-known Webster family of Kendal,[3] whose architects Francis and George have been recorded in Geoffrey Beard's book. He usually refers to Francis as Mr. Architect Webster. 16th December 1813 "... went to Mr. Architect Websters, he was from home, but Mrs. Architect was there entertaining company — cold of my feet and uncomfortable I returned to the White Hart spending my time with Mr. Richardson the drawing master — till Mr. Lishman came." Richardson and Lishman[4] were both local artists and teachers of art. This subject was one of those most popular with young ladies and considered essential for their education. Most of these names appear on his subscribers' lists to his series of prints.

Whatever their opinion of him he was clearly in touch with other artists, as in April 1808 he complains bitterly of not being able to get on with his painting because of other artists coming to see his work.

There are several appreciative remarks about him by members of the literary and artistic circle. Christopher North, a great admirer and friend to Green, said he was "the most sober and industrious of God's creatures". Hartley Coleridge was one of his devoted friends and admirers and said "Of all landscape painters he was the most literal, the most absolute copyist of the objects on his retina. What he saw he painted as exactly as could be painted but he certainly knew when to catch each view in its most romantic moment. He knew the trees and waterfalls as well as he knew his own children. He was not a man to belie the magnificent world for the credit of his craft. He loved truth too well. He had a hearty, healthy love of his employment such as none but an honest man could feel or understand. He taught his pencil too, as he taught his children, — to speak the truth. His landscapes convey a direct corporeal perception in its very picture, circumstance and complexion of the instant."

Green said the Duddon was "the vale that was the darling of his heart." His daughter Jane once said, "You will excuse my father's enthusiasm for his darling art, he knows no other world than that in which a painter lives" ... "his spirit never flagged, his hand and eye were never idle." "A lover of nature, he was no lover of solitude, and like many whose occupations condemn them to long silences, he seized eagerly on all opportunities of conversation." "He loved to talk the country dialect, and was welcome at all farms as friend", wrote Canon Rawnsley in the nineteenth century.

But the greatest praise perhaps came from William Wordsworth, who wrote the epitaph for Green's gravestone. In the *Letters of Dorothy and William Wordsworth*, (edited by Alan Hill, second edition 1806-11), is a letter to Sir George Beaumont by William Wordsworth. "I have purchased a black lead Pencil Sketch of Mr. Green of Ambleside which I think has great merit, the materials being uncommonly picturesque and well put together; I should dearly like to have the same subject (it is the Cottage at Glencoyn, by Ullswater) treated by you."

Also there is another letter (Wordsworth Letters 1812-1820) when he mentioned that one of Green's daughters taught art.

Finally, after Green died, Dorothy Wordsworth helped Green's son to find a job. The following correspondence shows how much trouble the Wordworths took over the boy.

*"Address:* John Marshall, Junr, Esqre, Headingly, Leeds.
*MS. WL.*
*LVi. 284*

Rydal Mount, near Kendal<br>December 23rd 1827

My dear Sir,
    You will, I hope, before this reaches you, have received a parcel *for your Mother* and directed *to your care,* which a Friend of mine, going to Leeds, was so kind as to take charge of. That parcel consists of two school-books, specimens of the hand-writing etc. of George Green, a Son of the late Mr. Green of

*Langdale Pikes.*

*Langdale Head from Wall End.*

Ambleside, and, if Mrs. Marshall be not yet arrived at Headingley, I beg you will be so kind as to open it, and look over the Books. I am aware that you are much more concerned in the matter, which I am going to lay before you, than your Mother, yet I should not have troubled you with it, except through her, had it not been of importance not to lose time.

A few weeks ago I wrote to inform your Mother and Aunts of the Death of Mr. Green's eldest unmarried Daughter, who was the main prop of the Family, and of a plan which had been set on foot for their relief by raising a Subscription, to which I received a most kind and satisfactory reply. But it is not on that subject that I address you.

Some years ago you kindly offered to take Hartley Green, an elder Brother of George into your Factory, which he declined, having other views. This circumstance encourages me to hope that you may, if you have any opening for such a youth, be willing to take *George,* who is exceedingly desirous of obtaining the situation — or indeed *any* situation which through industry and a desire of improvement may hereafter insure a creditable independence; but, above all things he seems to wish that it may be possible for you to take him into a situation similar to that which was offered to his Brother.

George Green will be sixteen years of age next March. From the Books which I have sent, you will be able to judge of his hand-writing and perhaps also of his progress in arithmetic. To this I will add that he is a Boy of modest and pleasing manners, and is in all respects very well thought of in Ambleside and the neighbourhood.

He is a dutiful Son and of very industrious habits. His Mother tells me that he is of a mechanical turn, and I know that he has made some progress in mathematics. He has, besides, always been reckoned a 'good Scholar' among the Schoolboys at the Grammar School at Ambleside: and has the appearance of being quick and clever. In short, there is something very prepossessing in this youth, with a pleasing modesty in his address.

Many kind Friends interest themselves in George Green's behalf, and I find that by this day's post an application has been made for a specimen of his hand-writing etc. and a hope held out of a situation (in a Counting house, I believe), but if you were willing to take him, and if it could be arranged in other points, he would greatly prefer being in your establishment to any thing else.

Hartley Green, the elder, is about to establish an academy at Manchester, and might find employment for his Brother, but he wishes rather to make his own way.

And now, my dear Sir, having said this much on behalf of this deserving Youth, I must beg to assure you that however zealous my wish to be the means of serving him and his poor Mother, I do not wish, *on that account,* to influence you — Quite the contrary — I know that in similar cases, your benevolent views have been disappointed, and, perhaps, you have consequently made arrangements for the Future which may render it ineligible to take any youth in the same way as proposed to his Brother — even if you have at present — or are likely in course of a year or two — to have a vacancy. At all events, I shall be much obliged to you if you will write to me as soon as possible — in order that, if you do not hold out any hope, he may not lose time, and if you do, that you may receive further information; and he be put into the way of preparing himself, according to your wishes, for the situation. I *ought* to have said, that though not a *stout* young man, he has always been very healthy, and has no dread of confinement.

Excuse this long letter and believe me, dear Sir, your affectionate Friend,

Dorothy Wordsworth."

[1]William Bellers was an artist who worked in the mid 18th Century, (1761-73 at the Free Society,) so whether this is the same print maker in his old age we cannot tell.

[2]*Harden Diary* transcript p. 11.

[3]Francis Webster 1767-1827, his sons George 1797-1864, Robert 1794-1810.

[4]Lishman painted local views and one of Abbot Hall, Kendal is now in the Art Gallery there. He was dancing and also drawing master at Ulverston and Kendal. He was listed in the local directory of 1834 as a landscape painter and lived in Castle Street, Kendal. He died in 1850.
John Richardson (1774-1864) was an architectural draughtsman who practised architecture in Kendal where he made a number of sketches of local buildings in watercolour. He was also responsible for designing several buildings in Kendal: Town View and the Shakespeare Theatre.

[5]*The Letters of William and Dorothy Wordsworth,* 2nd ed., *III The Later Years Part One, 1821-1828,* revised, arranged and edited by Alan G. Hill, O.U.P., 1978, pp. 562-563.

# Chapter 7

# The Guide Books

When Green began writing his Guide Book to the Lake District these aids to walkers had already become popular. The ever increasing army of tourists who came up to look at the scenery was growing. The very scenery which had at first terrified people as recorded by Gilpin and others was steadily becoming attractive to visitors. The idea that people needed to be shown from where to view the lakes, hills and mountains developed into the "stations" or points from which to see the best views to the best vantage. Later readers were often puzzled by the references to "stations" at a time long before the first arrival of the railway in Cumbria.

Green's text in these and in his series of black and white pictures of the area was usually restricted to straightforward descriptions of the places portrayed or of the directions to reach them. Occasionally however more personal comments creep in such as in his 1814 publication, *A Description of Sixty Small Prints* where on page 17 he wrote "Skiddaw has been called a generous Lord, and the Fells of Borrowdale frowning and haughty Tyrants. Are frowning and haughty tyrants to be preferred to generous Lords? Man in his feelings towards man has now pretty well made up his mind on that head; but in his choice of mountains probably he may like the tyrant best."

He was often thoughtful for the traveller, offering him the easiest path for walking. "The artist has commenced his Description at Coniston Water, and pursued a line which he thinks will have less to be retraced than any other he could have chosen."

Energy must have abounded in the early walkers. He recommended one walk to those who would avoid being tired — Borrowdale, Buttermere, Newlands, Rosthwaite, Keswick, a mere 23 miles.

Already prone in his diaries to use the superlative it was indeed somewhat of a problem in trying to entice people to see the beauties of the Lake District, not to use repeatedly such expressions as "the grandest view of all", "one of the finest assemblages in England", over and over again.

His words as well as his paintings however evoked atmosphere. Gillerthwaite — "was under the influence of a warm and sportive sunshine, which rendering lazy, while it illuminated the lowing herds of cattle, presented, to the mind's eye, after their viewing such a scene the results of a Cuyp, a Bergham, or a Potter, or of many an English painter of animals."

Mr. Gilpin said "picturesque ideas are all cloathed in bodily forms, and may often be explained better by a few strokes of the pencil than by a volume of the most laboured description." Green realized he was better with the pencil than writing but made his excuse "were his information for the satisfaction of an individual only, he would prefer the former as a vehicle for information, but to give to the public a numerous series of explanations all cloathed in bodily forms; besides time and other minor considerations, it is necessary to consult the copper smith, the printer, and the paper merchant." He was also aware that his writing might act as a "soporific to closet readers."

On February 3rd 1817 an entry in his diary hints at the dreariness he found in his marathon task of writing the Guide. "Began writing" for three days, but on 8th, "Went to Mr. Lishman — drank tea at his father's a mighty lift to writing."

Yet he could convey his feelings about the country with real emotion, as in the extract from his description of Cockley Beck.[1]

The Guide Book came out in two volumes in 1819. It included a map by Jonathan Otley printed by Menzies in Edinburgh.

"KENDAL: Printed and Published, by R. Lough and Co. and Sold by them at the Chronicle Office, Finkle Street: also by J. Richardson, 91, Royal Exchange, London; Constable, Edinburgh; Smith, Liverpool; Messrs. I. Clark, and Co. Manchester; Wilcockson, Preston; Dewhurst, Lancaster; Foster,

# WESTMORLAND ADVERTISER

## and

## KENDAL CHRONICLE

No. 437     8th Week Qr.                    Saturday, November 6, 1819

THIS DAY IS PUBLISHED,

In Two large Octavo Volumes, containing together
1,000 Pages of Letter Press,

## A DESCRIPTION

of the

## LAKES & MOUNTAINS

in

Cumberland, Westmorland & Lancashire,

### WITH SOME ACCOUNT OF THEIR BORDERING TOWNS AND VILLAGES

The result of Observations made during a Residence
of upwards of 18 Years in Ambleside and Keswick.

— — — — — — —

## BY WILLIAM GREEN

oOo

SIXTEEN Years of the above period were appropriated to the production of Drawings and Sketches, from the prominent to the most retired features of this interesting district; but the three last years have been principally devoted to numerous excursions, made with the design of collecting materials to be exhibited in a series of directions for the use of Tourists. The work will be interspersed with remarks on the present appearance of the Vallies, particularly as beautified or deformed by wood, or as connected by neighbouring elevations with more removed objects.

— — — — — — —

The price of the Work, with a Map and 12 Prints, One Guinea. — On a superior Paper, with a Map and 24 Prints, Two Guineas.

— — — — — — —

The Author requests of those Ladies and Gentlemen who have already done him the favour of subscribing to the Work that they will again signify their intentions, as it is feared that some of their names may have been omitted in the Subscription Book.

Please to address the AUTHOR, in Ambleside, or Mr. LOUGH, at the Printing Office, Kendal.

— — — — — — —

On the same day will be ready for delivery, a Box, containing Ten Large Cups of Original Colour, and Four Compounds; prepared under the direction of WILLIAM GREEN. An introduction to the Study of Mountain Landscape, is written and will be published with these Colours.

The Compounds are calculated to save much valuable time, for by their agency the eight preparatory Tints may be produced with greater certainty in five minutes, than can be done from the original Colours in an hour.

The explanation of the Colours and the Compounds is illustrated in the body of the Letter Press by a numerous arrangement of Tints, with their application to the Publisher's mode of proceeding through all the various stages of a Drawing.

The above Colours in large Mahogany Boxes, with the Letter Press, are £2 and £2.10s.

Ambleside, October 1st, 1819.

*Ennerdale.*

Kirkby Lonsdale; Ashburner, Ulverstone; Gaythorpe, Whitehaven; Jollie, Scott, and Thurnam, Booksellers, Carlisle; Shaw, Penrith; Bateman, Appleby; M. & R. Branthwaite, Dowson, Gritton, Todhunter, and Messrs. Bellingham and Airey, Kendal, and by the Author, at Ambleside. 1819."

Once he had decided to write the Guide Book he realised he would have to do a considerable amount of writing and although he never felt he was a good writer, his unwavering intent carried him through. Conscious of his literary failings he often pointed out that he wished some "literary residents, who by their good taste and frequent travel" could have undertaken the task. He often apologised for his English and also for the fact that this handy guide turned into two volumes. (Compared with a slim modern Wainwright the 2 volumes are quite heavy).

He used some of his text already published in his Sixty Etchings of 1814 and began early in 1816 to compile the Guide. He was at pains to point out that he had lived in Ambleside since 1800 and therefore knew the region intimately. The main features were well known to most travellers, but Green wanted them to discover the lesser known tarns, valleys and fells of his beloved Lake District. He hoped the Guide would "relieve the traveller from the burthen of those tedious enquiries on the road or at the inns, which generally embarrass and often mislead." The best time to see the Lakes he felt was not necessarily high summer, and he recommended people to come at all times of the year so that they might appreciate the great torrents of water after rain and misty light on cloudy days. "Books, drawing and music may, however, considerably alleviate the feeling of the suffering female during rainy weather." "Days of deluge" he said, "offered at least the consolation of eventual dry clothes" in which the walker could boast to his friends of the glories of his rambles round the fireside. In fact the only excuse for not going out in every weather was if sharp edges were to be negotiated to caverns, and this, he warned for safety reasons.

There is aptly from the pen of an artist a detailed description of the lead mines where the pencil lead was dug at Gillercoom;

"The entrance to the lower mine, is by a level of two hundred and twenty yards in length, which communicates with a shaft, one hundred yards deep. 'There are no certain marks on the surface to direct the miner, nor any regular stratum of this mineral.' It lies in sops or bellies, surrounded by hard rocks, which will readily account for its being suddenly lost; and these sops or bellies, being generally at considerable distances, will equally well account for the difficulty with which it is commonly regained . . ."

" 'The mineral is described, as sometimes lying in the mine in form resembling a tree.' The root or body of the tree is the finest lead, from which, it gradually becomes worse, as it approaches the extremities of the branches."[2]

The daring actions of slaters, copper and lead and iron miners were described, bringing to life those now deserted valleys throughout the centre of the area which must once have been hives of industry. The miners tramped up the valleys in the morning, worked all day and came down at night. Now only the deserted mine stores, gunpowder huts and relics of old machinery remind us of this former industrial occupation of the valleys and hills.

Inevitably he was drawn into historical references in his rather fulsome descriptions of sites such as Furness Abbey. At the time of his writing Barrow was a hamlet popular for bathers and with two large inns. He quoted much from previous writers of guides such as West and Close. Even religion and politics were subjects he covered in his preamble in relation to local inhabitants such as George Fox. He quoted at length from Richard Cumberland in the *European Magazine* of 1803 on the artist George Romney. In the midst of his writings he used suddenly to include advertisements for some of his editions of prints already published, adding for good measure that "His Highness the Prince Regent" had already ordered copies of the same.

In all his wanderings it is clear that the artist really preferred the Ambleside area. His familiarity with every stick and stone of it probably helped him to this preference. But as we have seen, he referred to the Duddon valley as "the darling of my heart" — he says in the Guide that Mr. West "contented himself by speaking of the scenery of easy access from the public roads, for he has entirely omitted the vast and romantic wilds which lie between the sea and the chain of lofty mountains, beginning at Coniston and ending at Lows Water — who shall traverse Seathwaite, Eskdale, Wastdale, Ennerdale and Ennersaledale, and not be ready to acknowledge that the Western side of his tour, though probably less beautiful, is infinitely more magnificent than the Eastern side?"

Dialect words fascinated him and footnotes were often added to help the reader on derivations of place-names and other unusual words. Indeed to the modern reader some of his vocabulary seems rather strange such as the word "umbrageous" in his description of the famous Yew Tree, "which is tall and beautiful, but not umbrageous like those at Patterdale," or "shivers" or "screeds" referring to screes. Other phrases sound archaic such as his "mazy windings", "sylvan softness" and "aerial atmosphere."

There are often interesting encounters with local people who either took him and his companions in, in bad weather, entertaining them with rum or milk, tea or dinner. Sometimes he would revert to a previous journey to a particular spot and described his personal experiences of several years before as in Vol I, pp. 111-113 when he describes how he had made sketches for plate Nos. 46, 47 and 49 of *Sixty Large Etchings*.

Innumerable short encounters were jotted down in his diaries, which he referred to as "memorandum books", as well as in the Guide Book. One of these referred to the old man who seemed to be the self-appointed guide to the Bowder Stone, that most popular tourist attraction, which hangs precariously, as it hung then, in Borrowdale. Apparently this old man, John Raven, lived in a shack beside the stone and made a good living out of selling a paper he had had printed, which gave the size, weight and origin of the stone. Various fairly unscientific theories have been put forward over the years as to why and how it got there. Mr. West had in fact calculated its weight to have been 1,771 tons.[3]

Green showed great sympathy for women, whose elaborate dress made climbing difficult:

"but an excess of out door ceremony *tended* and still tends to prevent the female from acquiring the proper use of her limbs, and of learning to bound from rock to rock with the celerity of the fleecy rangers of the mountains."

There was a description of the "three interesting females" who nearly lost their lives on the hills[4]. However women apparently fared better on horseback:

"A lady of light weight may ride to the top of Skiddaw without alighting, and descend it to the town in safety; if in the steepest parts someone manages her horses head. But it is a relief to both the rider and the horse occasionally to dismount."[5]

Of Stock Ghyll force Ambleside about which he was in high praise:

"The finest views are from the bottom, and at some places a little above it; but few dare venture to the bottom, particularly those females whose pedestrian excursions have chiefly been upon level ground; nay the male sex are often appalled with a view of the way, and many a Bond-street gentleman, in his stable costume, would rather hazard his neck four-in-hand, than risk it by having his arms precariously supported by the twigs and branches he may find in his way to the gulph below."[6]

Even Green did wonder why a better path could not have been made and recommended a little landscaping of trees and rocks which blocked the views of Stock Ghyll force.

Also the ghost stories of certain houses came in for comment and there is a long note on the haunting of Calgarth Hall. He described in detail the amazing story of strange sightings of vast armies of people seen at Midsummer's Eve at midnight often referred to as the Ghost Troops marching on Souter Fell[7].

Green, despite his modesty over his literary failings amidst his now rather ponderous descriptions, does achieve some delightful images in words:

"Twilight, in the absence of the moon, is a fine, a most interesting period. The sun illuminating the canopy of heaven, reflects its lustre on the earth below, and gives a delicate distinction to every distance on the picture, and to every object its due place, in all the regular gradation of aerial perspective."

"What can be more refreshing to the feelings of an artist, than to observe the localities of colour subdued and almost amalgamated with the floating atmosphere; the fore-ground in chastened tones and tints, and the distances swimming in celestial blue?"

"Surrounded by the melancholy gloom of night, how different the views of the artist and lover to those of the 'lean unwashed artificer' who at the very moment greedily swallowing sedition is all agog to hurl destruction on his rulers, who in their turns are as anxiously providing means to prevent its execution."

"In mild cloudy weather the vapour on the mountains sometimes travels horizontally, by which their summits are hid from the eye of the anxious spectator; but when ascending or descending mists shall roll upon the surface of gigantic nature, when some castle-like rock alternately of the deepest air tint and most celestial light, shall seem as hung in clouds, the powers of the pencil are frequently suspended, and the mind employed in comparing the greatness of nature with the littleness of art."[8]

His attitude here indicates perfectly his immense modesty and humility before the powerful landscape all around him.

*Stock Gill Force.*

Delightful phrases brighten his text, as "midnight murkiness," "visionary gratification," "delightful dingle, darkened by a profusion of oak trees," "useless hills," "uncontaminated nature," "picturesque assemblages" (usually referring to trees, cottages and weather); such words held the secrets of appreciating the Lake District in all its forms. He is really surprised that some people left the Lake District disgusted by the rainy weather. But "artists like sailors — if they expect to be gratified by rare sights — must pay the price." "Strangers usually retiring with the butterflies are seldom seen in October."

[1]*Guide Book,* Vol I, p. 110 ff: "...from Cockley Beck by Black Hall to Goldrill crag, which is about two miles, the scenery improves at every step; but not the river, which though occasionally frothy, is upon the whole tamely featured, and lazy. At Goldrill crag it brightens into agitation, and, after various changes, becomes at Wallowbarrow crag one scene of rude commotion, forming in its course a succession, not of high, but finely formed, water-falls; but these furious waters suddenly slumbering, become entranced, displaying little signs of life along the pleasant plains of Dunnerdale..."
"From Nettleslack Bridge, after a hasty dinner at the inn, the writer proceeded to Wallowbarrow crag, where he made three drawings, and No. 47 of the small etchings is one of them."
"Out of the bed of the river at the foot of Goldrill crag rises a prodigious stone, on each side of which the waters rush into a quiet pool below — from the receding rocks project trees, not profusely, but elegantly:..... The artist and his friend passed some time on the stone above mentioned, and happily without any injury: in the dead of the following night an immense fragment of Goldrill crag fell upon that stone; — had this happened at the time they were upon it, they must inevitably have fallen sacrifices to one of the objects of their admiration."

[2]*Guide Book,* Vol II, p. 165

[3]*Guide Book,* Vol II, p. 132

[4]*Guide Book,* Vol II, p. 241

[5]*Guide Book,* Vol II, p. 327

[6]*Guide Book,* Vol I, p. 157

[7]*Guide Book,* Vol II, pp. 449-451

[8]*Guide Book,* Vol I, pp. 76-77

# Chapter 8

# Social Needs and
# Green's Garden City Movement

In his books Green shows a strong social awareness of a liberal Georgian kind. He makes a point of mentioning in his Guide the provision (or lack of it) for the poor and ill. He saw the need for education in most of the small towns, and in Ambleside suggested plans for the employment of the workless. This scheme was part of a larger plan to provide better facilities for the "Lakers" as the tourists were called. Throughout the guide there is advice to all property owners on how to improve the aesthetic appearance of their estates. He almost invariably added that any expense would soon be made good by the increased value of the property. He had a good Mancunian's sense of 'brass'. He deplored the loss of work the machine looms were causing in the small lake towns and consequently "the production of individual misery." [1] So Hawkshead had lost the "animated cheerfulness" of its market day. At Hawkshead there used to be a famous market but after the invention of spinning machinery its importance declined. He was however thoroughly in favour of the right development of machines and suggested that machinery should be introduced to some rural communities to take the place of hand looms. "This created an animated cheerfulness, now lost and almost forgotton; but, shall the introduction of engines for the abridgement of manual labour, tend to the production of individual misery? God forbid!" Kendalians were described, a population of 8,000 as " a frugal, industrious people, and many of them have risen to a considerable degree of opulence by their assiduous attention to business."

Social needs always concerned him. For example his comments on a visit to Gillerthwaite confirm this attitude. "A more sylvan bottom than Gillerthwaite (Ennerdale) can scarcely be imagined." "A woman and her grandson were the only persons at Gillerthwaite when the writer was there." "The situation and the fertility of this bottom gave rise to reflections touching the present state of the labouring classes, who, in dungeon-like cellars, and bye allies, eke out a miserable existence, while with infinitely greater comfort to themselves, and honour and profit to the affluent, they might enjoy, in vast happiness, such peaceful and sequestered abodes as Gillerthwaite." [2]

Another social problem which concerned him was the lack of housing both for the poor and for the tourists. He even outlined a scheme to overcome these.

". . . at Low Wood, a mile and a half from Ambleside on the Kendal road, there is a pleasant and commodious inn, having post-chaise and good horses."

"In Ambleside there are several lodging houses, but it is a matter of surprise to the writer that there are not a greater number, as during the travelling season, when all such houses are full, more are enquired for by those who wish to see the country apart from the bustle, not to speak of the expence, of an inn. Furnished houses, pleasantly planted, would soon be tenanted, and private property enhanced in value by the consequent introduction of strangers."

"Few projects for amending the condition of the needy, and for the reduction of parish rates, would be so beneficially devised as to build lodging houses in places where they were likely to be let: and in what way could money be more securely deposited than by a general subscription, in shares of fifty or one hundred pounds each: five thousand pounds would build a number of houses, worth from five to twenty-five pounds per annum, or double that sum if furnished." [3]

What he was envisaging may even be compared with a modern community centre with craft centres and other amenities. Perhaps West who had been very conscious of social needs, had had an influence on his thoughts on such matters. The season was short for tourists in Green's time and he said that the expensively equipped inns made a frugal living in the two months of the year when they were busy, while for the rest of the year, no one came.

Tourism as such did not begin to flourish until the end of the 18th century. Robbery enough existed near London, but Southerners may have suspected, especially after the Jacobite Rebellion of 1715, that there was no order or security in the North and so not worth the long, expensive journey there. The roads were bad and hotels poor; in a Kentmere caravanserai in 1820 according to the *Lonsdale Magazine,* there is a good description of a mixture of farmhouse and public house, serving as hotel: "The floor was bespread with tubs, pans, chairs, tables, piggins, dishes, tins and the other equipage of a farmer's kitchen. In the dusk of the evening and the darkness of the house, the things were only just visible... innumerable obstacles that intervened between us and the cosy *hearth.* A robust girl, in a short petticoat of Kendal green... pushed the tubs and pots aside, and by that means formed a very tolerable avenue to the fire." There follows a description of the austere conditions for travellers. But when the inns did begin to improve they brought a great influx of visitors and by 1817[4] an observer remarks: "Thirty years earlier simplicity and hospitality were then the character of the people... Even the innkeepers treated their guests with a hospitality independent of self-interest, and the charges,... exceedingly moderate... The great influx of strangers... destroyed the original character of the natives. The innkeepers... made a wonderful progress in the arts of trade... At Keswick and Ambleside private (costs for) lodgings are much higher than what the same conveniences could be had for in London, Liverpool or Manchester". Bouch cannot vouch for this but suggests the number of visitors might have exceeded the available accommodation which in turn put prices up. Naturally the coach roads were the worst affected, while off the beaten track Green and no doubt others, continued to enjoy the former hospitality and generosity. By 1844, when Wordsworth so fiercely objected to the coming of the railway, many more people were being attracted not just for the natural attributes of the area but for all those extra attractions which were suddenly being introduced such as "wrestling, horse and boat races, and pot-houses and beer-shops."

Green was one of the forerunners of the Garden City Movement[5]. Looking back at it now this is perhaps the most imaginative part of the Guide Book and his progressive ideas positively amaze us. He saw the possibility of "an ideal residential paradise" on the south side of Keswick. This land, part of the Derwentwater estate, belonged to Greenwich Hospital. It was his idea that it would become a model city at an initial cost of £100,000. This was to be raised by various subscribers who would be limited to buying twenty shares each. The rentals would go to a common fund for the upkeep of the estate and for the improvement of land and forest. The houses were to be built at a pre-arranged cost and the architectural detail of each was to be carefully considered.

Haberdashers and provision merchants were to be granted a few houses. Some were to be tenanted by cooks, washerwomen, labourers and grooms. A tavern, dinner house, concert room and assembly room were to be provided. The city was to include one hundred and twenty-six furnished houses from £250 to £4,000 each and one hundred and seventy-four unfurnished houses from £62 to £200. Most important of all was to be the church, costing £10,000, which was to dominate the whole.

Green suggested that within this city the window tax should not apply. He believed that the tax destroyed the architectural merit of the houses. The subscribers ought to be allowed the "free entrance of light into these their pleasure houses as it steals from heaven without embargo or blockade."

Of more general interest Green emphasised the importance of woodlands in his residential paradise. He saw trees "as objects of local elegance and grandeur" and these should be held sacred. Such a well placed and well managed woodland would bring "never failing fountains of delight" to the inhabitants. He even offered advice to Greenwich Hospital who owned much of the land nearby on how to manage it.

The construction of villages where beds could be had by tourists for more than just the two months of July and August was advocated in suitably selected places. These included the treeless spaces north and south of Brocklebeck; he recommended places sheltered from the northern blast and with "commanding prospects of that noble lake," "the hollow between Derwent Park and Castlehead, and the fields extending from Castlehead to Keswick." Such improvements required not only the consent of the Governors of Greenwich Hospital, but also of Parliament.

"A sum less than one hundred thousand pounds would be inadequate to the full accomplishment of this desirable project. Five hundred thousand pounds would not only concentrate the skill of the empire on this very spot, but furnish the means of rendering similar accommodation, though on an inferior scale, at many distant places. Perhaps one hundred and fifty thousand pounds would be sufficient, and subscribed in shares of one hundred pounds, might be raised without difficulty. If subscribers were limited each to twenty shares the greatest possible number would be 1,500, and the least 75."

He thought it unwise to take the land by force but felt that the scheme if carried out properly would soon recompense all the subscribers. He even gave budgets for the plans showing the total costs of the proposed houses, furnished or unfurnished and with gardens. Everything was thought out, church, hospital and parks with benches*. After dealing with all other natural and visual amenities he concluded with his plans for a forest of oak, ash, beech and larch, little glades of flowers, railings painted with "invisible green", occasionally steps to be cut in steep rocks and handrails made of oak or larch to be installed. Waterfalls and cascades from high rocks and pools would be needed. Any deformity should be improved — such as "that disgusting row of ash trees extending from Friar Crag over Strands Hagg" which he wanted to turn into three irregular groups. There was, he pointed out, masses of stone and timber for building materials and firewood in abundance. Round, elliptical or other shelters, from which to admire the views, were to be installed in the woods in optimum sites for shelter. There would have to be wardens patrolling the area and they might like to serve teas "for wines and spirits by transforming men into woodland bacchanalians, might engender terror in the delicate frames of women, children, and others."

Unfortunately all Green's plans came to naught. The plans were sent to the Governors of the Greenwich Hospital, but they gave him no encouragement. As Rawnsley suggests in his book *By Fell and Dale at the English Lakes* (1911) with "our own little Garden City of Keswick" and others at Letchworth, Hampstead and Ruislip, Green was in this very much before his time. William Wordsworth may have been influenced in his ideas of development by William Green.

Perhaps it is as well the Guide Book ends at this point as he was then wondering, if further accommodation was needed when the fulfilment of the first scheme was achieved, about "approaches to many other favourite points of vision on side grounds or from the tops of mountains, ought next to engage the attention of the subscribers." But to be fair to Green it was from his burning wish for people to admire the scenery, not from a desire to spoil it, that he made these suggestions, which certainly are not so far fetched in the 20th century as they must have been then. The National Trust, Friends of the Lake District and the National Parks have put into practice many of Green's ideas, but the extent of his plans went even further than these and might well be worth looking at again. The plans he envisaged included the amenities for local people as well as for the tourists.

The Derwentwater estates were eventually sold and in February 1832 William Wordsworth wrote a letter saying:

"I often think how poor Mr. Green would have trembled for the issue, as the passing of this beautiful Property with many hands may exceedingly disfigure a neighbourhood, which he poor man often busied his hand in beautifying."[6]


*He planned that the visitors who would stay in the garden city would come by ship from the South and Ireland, to Manchester and Liverpool. He envisaged a 5 mile canal from Newby Bridge down to the navigable part of the Leven to help with transport.

[1]*Guide Book,* Vol I, p. 120

[2]*Guide Book,* Vol II, p. 237

[3]*Guide Book,* Vol I, pp. 150-151

[4]C. M. L. Bouch & G. P. Jones *The Lake Counties 1500-1830. A Social & Economic History.* Manchester University Press. 1961.

[5]*Guide Book,* Vol II, pp. 475-495

[6]*The Letters of William and Dorothy Wordsworth,* 2nd ed., 1829-1834 p.494.

## Chapter 9

# His Love of Nature and Local Colour

*Raven Crag.*

Green loved the landscape of the Lake District and frequently said it was "full of courteous invitation to the artist." Crummock he once described "This grand concatenation of parts." When lost for words he occasionally quoted other people's descriptions of the scenery.

"Between the top of Skiddaw and the Lake of Bassenthwaite the numerous narrow openings are happily described by Housman . . . 'on looking down the profound precipice in almost any direction the eye recoils with horror. Chasms of enormous depths in the bowels of the mountain forming steeps of slaty shiver yawn upwards with frightful grin.' Green added "it is an amusing sort of exercise to tramp along the edges of these grinning fissures."[1]

Many artists have revelled in drawing or painting trees. Green not only loved painting them but actually loved trees for themselves and for their beauty in the landscape. He deplored indiscriminate tree cutting, as we have seen.

He did not hesitate to give his own views on the subject. The collected volume of his *Seventy eight studies from Nature* (1809) contains an 8-page discourse entitled 'A Few Observations with respect to the mode in which Plantations ought to be Conducted.' He admired gnarled oak, beeches and silver birch, but occasionally he complained bitterly about bad planting, as when looking towards Langdale from near Tilberthwaite: "Langdale on the right would finish the whole into a pleasant landscape, were it not for a frightful plantation of firs blotting out the pass on Wrynose."[2] Also Landseer came to Green's rescue on this, his favourite subject, and wrote in the *New London Review,* "It does not appear that the landed proprietors among these mountains, feel a necessity for improvements of this sort, by the havoc that is displayed in the felling of their woods and coppices." He gave sound advice to the proprietors, that they should encourage and leave favourite trees to reach full maturity — "on every estate at least as many trees as acres"... "causing utility and beauty to go hand in hand." He thought Grasmere could have been infinitely more beautiful with more judicious planting.[3]

"Beauty depends on the multitude of its land owners; for were Grasmere the property of one person, he might exterminate the wood in a spring; but fifty men are seldom in one humour. The genius of this country imperiously demands a true taste, or no taste at all, in which case every farm within twenty miles of Langdale Pikes should have a different landlord."... "True taste does not in conspicuous places, exhibit large plantations or lumps of evergreens in circles, in squares, parallelograms,... nor often in rows."[4] Green continues: "Strangers have done more for the beauty of Grasmere by their forbearance in felling native trees than injury by the introduction of exotics."[5] "The Churchyard of Grasmere... is interesting... some charitable stranger has lately added the mournful yew, a tree sacred to such situations."[6]

He praised the Bishop of Llandaff for his enlightenment as a land owner but the Bishop, who lived at Calgarth, was an enthusiastic planter of larch trees. In a letter of 1794 he wrote: "Yet the highest and most craggy parts, two acres of which do not afford sustenance for six months to one sheep, might, with a great prospect of success, be planted with larches." And in 1818: "I made, in 1805 and 1806, a large plantation consisting of three hundred and twenty-two thousand five hundred larches, on two high and barren mountains, called Berkfell and Gomershow, situated near the foot of Winandermere." Tree planting and the good management of estates and forests had become very important by the end of the 18th century. "The Colpoy's Commission of 1805 reported that the woods about Keswick were in excellent order and managed with great care and attention."[7] Curwen stated that larches were first planted at Unerigg in 1780, at Workington in 1786 and on Belle Isle in 1787. He planted oaks also, 14 acres in 1794. "Altogether he planted on the slopes of Windermere over a million trees, 'Curwen's Woods'." "In 1809 he won the Society of Arts gold medals, having planted in a single year over a million larches and other forest trees" — he planted for posterity.

Green recalled with amusement one owner's precaution to protect his trees near Keswick.

"The fruits of the park have been guarded latterly, not by a dragon, but by fierce bulls, one of which drove from his labours a celebrated artist, who, with difficulty, escaped over the wall into the lower park."[8]

He does not name the artist. In contrast, he also describes vandalism near Keswick, where:

"From Castlerigg brow, the fells of Newlands were admirably contrasted with the ancient road — Nothing is left, root and branch is exterminated; and thus a few of the most lovely acres in the universe, have been despoiled for an exchange of corn and grass, while millions infinitely better fitted for the sustenance of man are almost wholly neglected.... miserable patches of green and brown, which pervade the denuded area, and now startlingly salute the traveller, on his way from Keswick and Brow Top to the fort of Castleriggs."[9]

"It is much to be regretted, that the owner of the Purse Crag should have cut down the beautiful trees, which served so wonderfully to enrich the prospects on this side of the water. The profit derived from their sale could not be very considerable, and the land, if to be sold, would be regarded as infinitely less valuable to the situation purchaser."[10]

Interestingly, Jane, his daughter, wrote about her father:

"Trees with him have no other use, but that of giving softness and effect to a picture. The meadows are created for foregrounds, and the hills were designed for distances. Rivers only roll along to brighten up the landscape, and cattle graze only to give life to his drawings. When, therefore, anything is out of place in a picturesque point of view, it excites his criticism, notwithstanding its utility in other respects."[11]

One of the legendary figures of the Lake District was the Beauty of Buttermere. She must have impressed Green for he gave eye-witness accounts of the so-called Sally of Buttermere and his various meetings with her in 1791 when she was but 14, again in 1792, 1794, and in 1798 when he felt an irresistible wish to revisit Buttermere. He went yet again in 1801, by then she had altered from the time when she had "full eyes, vermillion lips, and cheeks like lillies"[12] to a "bulky wife of a farmer, blessed with much good humour and a ready utterance."

Captain Budworth, in the first edition of his *A Fortnight's Ramble,* was the means of bringing Mary (Sally of Buttermere) into notice. "Had it not been for that publication Sally might have avoided that almost overwhelming sea of troubles which resulted from harmlessly intended praise." But Budworth was an honest man, and, as such, felt a compunction for the errors in which he might have unthinkingly involved the innocent and unsuspecting female. Thus, in 1798, he re-visited Buttermere and met Sally with an intent to destroy the false consequence, which, in the breast of Sally, might have been sown by himself and germinated by others. He met Sally and told her he knew the author of *A Fortnight's Ramble* and, indeed, revealed his identity. He told her "I wrote it; and rejoice in having had such an opportunity of minutely observing the propriety of your behaviour. You may remember, I advised you, in that book, never to leave your native valley. Your age and situation require the utmost care. Strangers will come and have come, purposely to see you, and some of them with very bad intentions. We hope you will never suffer from them; but, never cease to be upon your guard. You really are not so handsome as you promised to be; and I have long wished, by conversation like this, to do away what mischief the flattering character I gave of you may expose you to. Be merry and wise." That some would come with very bad intentions proved the truth and a person under the assumed character of a man of rank deceived and married the unsuspecting Sally but he did not survive his villanies. A general respect towards her grew out of her sufferings; having borne them with humility, she judiciously re-settled in her native valley. Again, she was addressed, but, by a man of character, and she settled, with her husband, in a distant part of Cumberland.

Green introduced some novel ideas perhaps reminiscent of pan pipes in earlier painting. On a part of Blakerigg at the foot of the gill from Blea Tarn there was a place with a fine echo, and Green imagined "Music amid such wilds! ah! how charming, plaintive solos on the clarinet or flute would have a fine effect amongst such rocks, which during the intervals of rest, would echo back the melancholy notes in soft reverberations, and produce in the mind a union of the most pleasing sensations."[13]

Bird watchers and most other people are delighted that the Golden Eagle, a native of these parts, is now beginning (with some difficulty) to nest and breed in the mountains. Green gave an interesting account of how this fine bird suffered at the hands of the sheep farmers who had lost lambs and so had to destroy it. Men, he said, used to approach the nest 60 yards down on a rope, and holding a piked stick in one hand to protect themselves from the parent birds' attacks, with the other hand seize the eggs or chicks, the latter was a valued object and the former they could sell for 5/- each. He told some gory stories of eagles carrying off dogs and lambs, of their being shot and maimed. This was in Borrowdale. He also mentioned the eagle in Buttermere with its struggle against gun and man. On one occasion he nearly saw the man killed: "The rope, sixty-five yards long, on his being drawn up, having a knot in the middle, was arrested by a clint (crack) in the rock, to which, with an eaglet sixteen and a half pounds weight, tied to his back, he had no other resource than that of ascending by his hands, the space something overhanging from the nest to the crack . . . The destruction of the parent birds was often attempted, by gun shot, but unsuccessfully, till from an ambush station, behind a stone, at the head of Buttermere Water, Mr. J. Vicars, nearly thirty years ago, shot at, and wounded both the eagles at the same time; one being descried immediately behind the other. The eagles were afterward found dead . . ."[14]

Natural phenomena intrigued him and in particular the "waterspouts" — which we now call flash-floods so frequent in very wet weather.

"To the untutored view a greater or more imposing display is necessary to afford pleasure. When a well proportioned quantity of water is passed over the unequal surface of a richly coloured rock, which thus aided, glows with borrowed brightness and augmented beauty on the delighted wanderer's gaze, the spectacle is replete with dazzling fascination, and the mind most avaricious of enjoyment can covet no more. Such has been the treat which here has occassionally fallen to the share of the writer, who has witnessed every appearance on this mountain's side, from the pretty timid water spout to the mighty roaring cataract. After successive days of heavy rain, the hollows before mentioned, become insufficient to receive the mighty volume of water which descends from the impending clouds upon them, and the maddening torrents are hurled from their rugged elevation with the awful roar of thunder: the grey rocks, occasionally tinted by pervading lichens, and still more beautifully enriched by many greened mosses resembling cushions of soft velvet, produce combinations of colour the most

*Derwentwater*

animated and superb, which, contrasted with the milky hue of the convulsed waters, form a picture of transcendent sublimity and beauty."[15]

The following interesting account of a waterspout which happened about the middle of the 18th century is copied from Mr. Hutchinson.

"This remarkable fall of water, which happened at nine o'clock in the evening of the 22nd of August, 1749, began with most terrible thunder, and incessant lightening, the preceding day having been extremely hot and sultry. The inhabitants, for two hours before the breaking of the cloud, heard a strange noise, like the wind blowing in the tops of high trees. It is thought to have been a spout, or larger body of water, which, by the lightening incessantly rarifying the air, broke at once on the tops of the mountains, and descended upon the valley below, which is about three miles long, half a mile broad, and lies nearly east and west, being closed on the south and north sides with prodigious high, steep, and rocky mountains..."[16]

Splendid and lurid descriptions of water spouts are recorded and included Gilpin's description of that of 1760:

"Grasmire and Whiteside are separated by a frightful chasm, which, fifty-eight years ago, was the channel of a tremendous water spout... Mr. Gilpin's description of this desolating water spout, will be read with interest, as combining great accuracy with language of uncommon elegance:

'On the 9th September, 1760, about mid-night, the water spout fell upon Grasmire, nearly as was conjectured, where the three little streams, just mentioned, issue from their mountains. At first, it swept the whole side of the mountain, and, charging itself with all the rubbish it found there, made its way into the vale, following chiefly the direction of the Lissa. At the foot of the mountain, it was received by a piece of arrable ground, on which its violence first broke. Here, it tore away trees, soil, and gravel, and laid all bare, many feet in depth, to the naked rock. Over the next ten acres, it seems to have made an immense fall, covering them with so vast a bed of stones, that no human art can ever again restore the soil.' "[17]

The buildings of the area also really interested him and those small grey stone houses nestling into the clefts and valleys have never been shown so naturally. His packhorse bridges and old barns were drawn without exaggeration.

He lamented the "modernizing" of the old buildings. In fifty years from then began the great wave of late Victorian building, which has so altered the appearance of places like Ambleside, especially if one compares old Church Street or the Market Place in Green's time, to 1860, and with what it has become today. To move forward to the present there would have been yet another shock for Green. Wordsworth shared Green's dislike of white rendered buildings in the Lake District.

He goes on to say that the main purpose of writing was to "save from the wreck of time and the busy hand of man the best specimens of this mountain architecture, is one of the principal objects of the present publication..." One and a half centuries later, similar books are being contemplated with text and photographs but the march of progress does not heed them. Yet in the Notes on his *78 Drawings from Nature* of 1809 he does relent a little. Drawing No. 78 has this comment: "This Plate exhibits one of these new buildings which afford comforts the poor inhabitants of the picturesque seldome enjoy; but it is but just to observe that the wealthy residents in Ambleside, natives and strangers, are exceedingly attentive to the wants of the needy, and supply them with a discriminating kindness that does equal honour to their heads and to their hearts."

Much of the Guide Book is taken up with careful description of colourful life in the Lake District. He described details that had been forgotten. It is a point of historical interest that after the Derwentwater's house was transferred to Dilston, the stone of the ancient castle which was on Castle Rigg[18], was used for a summer residence on Lord's Island; by 1711 this house was also flattened. Lord Derwentwater was beheaded in 1716. The Royal Oak had belonged to the Derwentwaters. Stones from the Island house were used to build the Town Hall in 1700. Green was all for restoring Lord's Island which seemed to have had a strange fascination for him, as it has for the present writer who has also, found for herself, the vestiges of the pier, the house, the shooting butts, etc.[19]

The *Histories of Cumberland,* by Dr. Burn, and Mr. Hutchinson, do not mention the time when Lord's Island, as a seat, was abandoned by the Radcliffe family. One thing is certain, that the last Lord Derwentwater, not long before his death, was frequently at Keswick, but according to Green it is not equally certain, that he then (as is affirmed by some) inhabited the house upon the island; on the contrary, it rather seems that his being at Keswick, was only on visits from his family place at Dilston.

Some of the delights of the area in the 18th century were the Regattas held from 1781-91. These took place on Derwentwater. A splendid description of one of these appeared in the Cumberland Pacquet of 1782 on the 6th September, and is quoted in his Guide:

" 'At eight o'clock in the morning, a vast concourse of ladies and gentlemen appeared on the side of Derwent Lake, where a number of marquees, extending about four hundred yards, were erected.' As the guests poured over in boats to Mr. Pocklington's island, by invitation, their landing was saluted by a discharge of artillery. When the noise died down a signal gun was fired and five boats pushed off from the shore and began the race. 'The sides of the hoary mountains were clad with spectators, and the glassy surface of the lake was variegated with numbers of pleasure barges, which, tricked out in all the gayest colours, and glittering in the rays of a meridian sun, gave a new appearance to the celebrated beauties of this matchless vale.' "

Then at about three o'clock a fleet of barges armed with cannon and muskets prepared for a sham attack on Pocklington's Island. "A terrible cannonading began on both sides, accompanied with a dreadful discharge of musquetry"... "All nature seems to be in an uproar, which impressed on the awakened imagination, the most lively ideas of the 'war of elements' and 'The crush of worlds'". After a severe conflict, the enemies were driven from their attack, in great disorder. So it continued, and ended with fireworks and dances at Keswick.[20]

Often alone, but on other occasions accompanied by his daughter Jane, Green really regarded the whole area as his home. In his long hours out of doors it was his world.

[1]*Guide Book,* Vol II, p. 340

[2]*Guide Book,* Vol I, p. 247

[3]*Guide Book,* Vol I, p. 264ff

[4]*Guide Book,* Vol I, p. 265

[5]*Guide Book,* Vol I, p. 263

[6]*Guide Book,* Vol I, p. 409

[7]Edward Hughes, *North Country Life in the Eighteenth Century,* Vol II, O.U.P., 1965, quoting Reports, 1808, 63 and 1810, 85.

[8]*Guide Book,* Vol I, p. 389

[9]*Guide Book,* Vol II, p.482-507

[10]*Guide Book,* Vol I, p. 345

[11]*Roeder*

[12]*Guide Book,* Vol II, pp. 180-185

[13]*Guide Book,* Vol I, p. 252

[14]*Guide Book,* Vol II, pp. 141, 214-215

[15]*Guide Book,* Vol I, p. 428

[16]*Guide Book,* Vol I, p. 429

[17]*Guide Book,* Vol II, p. 205

[18]*Guide Book,* Vol II, p. 464

[19]*Guide Book,* Vol II, p. 71 ff

[20]*Guide Book,* Vol II, pp. 85-89

this beautiful scenery
— interest the people
of Liverpool and Man
chester in the affair
& it will be certain
to answer, get a num
ber of the wealthy to
subscribe one guinea
or less each — & let
such people only or
purchasers to the amount
of ten guineas be eligi
ble to see the Sketches.
returned home by the
public high way & not

# Appendix I

# Works by William Green as recorded by Roeder

1794    Plan of Manchester. £2 2s.

1796    "A series of Picturesque Views of the North of England, drawn from nature and engraved by Wm. Green," consisting of forty-eight views of the Lakes, price £12. 12s 6d. (Announced in *Manchester Mercury* 19th January, 1796, number 2,317) 21½in by 16½in. Done 1794.

A Description of a Series of Picturesque Views in the North of England, printed at G. Nicholson and Co's office, 4, Palace Street 1796. (This is in the Manchester Reference Library.)

1796    Four Views of Wales, aquatinted, price £1 11s. 6d.; drawn, aquatinted, and published by W. Green, Lad Lane, Manchester. (One of the set in possession of Mr. Geo. Middleton, Ambleside.)

1799    Castle Street, Liverpool, illuminated by the great fire at Messrs Wakefield and O'Kill's sugar-house, which happened May 22nd, 1799, painted by J. Fernel, engraved by W. Green, 74, Charlotte Street, Portland Place, London.

1800-
1807    Finished Pencil Drawings of Lake Views, 26in. by 19in. (Some in possession of Mr. W. H. Mayson).

1804    A Set of Views in Mezzotint. (One of the set in possession of Mr. G. Middleton, Ambleside.)

1808    Thirty Studies from Nature, etched in the soft ground, by Wm. Green, Ambleside, after drawings made by himself in Cumberland, Westmorland, and Lancashire, dated 24th June; drawn and engraved and published by W. Green; 30in. by 21in. and 26in. by 19in.

1809    Guide Book.

1809    Twelve Studies from Nature, etched in the soft ground, by Wm. Green, Ambleside, after drawings made by himself in Cumberland, Westmorland, and Lancashire, dated 1st August; drawn and engraved and published by W. Green; 30in. by 21in.

1809    Seventy-eight Studies from Nature, engraved by Wm. Green from drawings by himself; Longman, Hurst, Rees, and Orme, London, and W. Green, Ambleside, published 1st August, 1809, with a preface, "A few observations with respect to the mode in which plantations ought to be conducted," pp. 13-20; oblong 4to, August 1st, price £5. 5s.; various sizes, 21in. by 14¾in. and 14¾in. by 11¾in. (One copy in Manchester Reference Library).

1810    Eighteen Studies from Nature, etched in the soft ground, by Wm. Green, Ambleside, after drawings made by himself in Cumberland, Westmorland, and Lancashire, dated 24th June; drawn and engraved and published by W. Green; 30in. by 21in.

1810    A Description of Sixty Studies from Nature (of the series of 1808, 1809, 1810); the price of the prints, unbound, including the description, 10 guineas; London, printed for the author by J. Barfield, and published by Longman, Hurst, Rees, and Orme, 1810. (One copy, Green's own apparently, in the Chetham Library, marked B9,53,35,216.) 122pp. and introduction. Of these Mr. Mayson has a fair number; various sizes exist.

1814    A Description of a Series of small Prints, etched by Wm. Green, of Ambleside, from drawings made by himself, London and Ambleside, with letterpress description, 1-34 pp., post 8vo, 9½in. by 7½in., dated August 1st; London, printed for the author by John Taylor, Rathbone Place, £1.5s.; the same appeared also aquatinted, same size.

1815   A series of Sixty beautifully coloured Plates of the Lakes of Lancashire, Cumberland, and Westmorland, drawn and engraved by W. Green, oblong folio, price £5 5s., dated 1st June (the fifth part of a projected series of 300 views). Same set in India ink, £3. 3s., 13½in. by 9½in. and 7in. by 4½in. Same set in printer's colours, £4. 4s., on 9to imperial. Same set etched, £1. 1s., on 8vo paper. Same set, etched, £1.5s., upon larger paper. (Two copies in possession of Councillor Henry Plummer.)

1819   The Tourists' New Guide, containing a description of the Lakes, Mountains, and Scenery in Cumberland, Westmorland, and Lancashire (the result of eighteen years' residence in Ambleside and Keswick), two volumes, Kendal, 1819. With twelve plates, £1. 1s., also done in sepia, dated 1st August 1819. With twenty-four plates, £2. 2s. (Some of the original drawings still in possession of Mr. Mayson.)

1819   Forty Views of Buildings and Bridges, etched, no date, but with watermark of 1819, 13½in. by 9¾in., of Ambleside, Keswick, etc.

1819   A Set of Etchings of Buildings in Ambleside, etc. (watermark 1819), undated, 22½in. by 17in.

1820   Twelve Coloured Prints of Views of the principal Lakes, published 1st August, 25in. by 17½in., £10. 10s.

1820   Sepia and Coloured Prints, dated June 1st, 22in. by 15in, £7. 10s. (twelve views of the Lakes).

1821   Twelve Coloured Views of the Lakes, dated June 1st, 12in. by 8½in., £3. 3s.

1821   Forty Views of Ambleside and Keswick, etched from nature, by Wm. Green, 21in. by 15in.

# Roeder also listed the whereabouts of some of Green's watercolours at that time:

| | |
|---|---|
| Langdale Pike | |
| Sprinkling Tarn | In seven stages. In |
| St. John's Vale | possession of Mr. Mayson |
| Yew Carron from Borrowdale | |
| Yew Carron and Gable, or Wast Water | |
| *Scafell on Wast Water | |
| *Derwent Water and Bassenthwaite in the distance | About 1808-9 |
| *One, subject not named | |
| Two Watercolour drawings, 19in. by 13in. | About same date |
| Old Bridge in Borrowdale, and two others in the British Museum | |
| Raven Crag, Thirlmere; in South Kensington. | |
| The Old Market House, Ambleside | Mrs. Walmsley, |
| The Old Commercial Hotel, Market Place | Ambleside |
| Same subjects, in possession of Mrs. Garside, Ambleside | |

*These were in 1882 in possession of his nephew, Mr. B. H. Green, Plas Fron Deg, Llandudno.

# *Appendix II*

# *Family Tree*

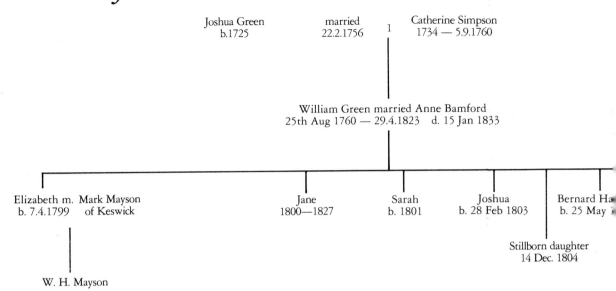

Joshua Green
b.1725

married
22.2.1756

1

Catherine Simpson
1734 — 5.9.1760

William Green married Anne Bamford
25th Aug 1760 — 29.4.1823   d. 15 Jan 1833

Elizabeth m.  Mark Mayson
b. 7.4.1799      of Keswick

Jane
1800—1827

Sarah
b. 1801

Joshua
b. 28 Feb 1803

Bernard Ha
b. 25 May

Stillborn daughter
14 Dec. 1804

W. H. Mayson

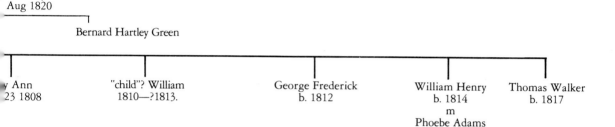

beth Hartley

d Hartley Green
Aug 1820

Bernard Hartley Green

| y Ann | "child"? William | George Frederick | William Henry | Thomas Walker |
| 23 1808 | 1810—?1813. | b. 1812 | b. 1814 | b. 1817 |
| | | | m | |
| | | | Phoebe Adams | |

## *William Green's Family*

William Green's father, Joshua Green, was a schoolmaster, and clerk of St. John's Church, Deansgate, Manchester.

William Green's step-brother, Bernard Hartley Green became a cotton merchant; he was an early Chairman of the Manchester Exchange and borough-reve of Salford. He had a son, also Bernard Hartley Green.

William Green was survived by nine children — four daughters and five sons, (see Family Tree). A sixth son died in infancy, and there was at least one still-birth.

Elizabeth married Mark Mayson of Portinscale, Keswick, on 3 February 1819; their son, W. H. Mayson became a well-known violin-maker in Manchester and author of *The Stolen Fiddle* (1897). He also provided Roeder with much of the information for his article.

Joshua was lost at sea, at some date after 1820 when he suffered his accident with gunpowder.

Bernard Hartley was a tutor of languages in Manchester, where he was "about to set up an academy" when Dorothy Wordsworth wrote to John Marshall junior on 23 December 1827.

Mary Ann became an art dealer in Liverpool.

George Frederick, for whom Dorothy Wordsworth tried to find employment in John Marshalls's factory in Leeds, eventually emigrated to Australia, whither he allegedly took the portrait of his father (in pigtail, wig and silver shoebuckles), which he had painted when he was a surveyor in Manchester. His great, great grandson, Mr. Purves of Melbourne, presented William Green's diaries to Abbot Hall Art Gallery.

William Henry became a wine merchant in Manchester. He married Phoebe Adams at Manchester Collegiate Church in 1840.

Thomas Walter worked as an engraver with (Robert?) Graves in London.

The "child" to whom Miss Weeton stood godmother on 11 October 1810 is very probably the William who was buried at Grasmere, 10 February 1813.

# Text of
# William Wordsworth's
# Epitaph to William Green

"Sacred to the memory of
William Green,
the last twenty-three years of whose life was passed,
in this neighbourhood
where, by his skill and industry as an artist
he produced faithful representations
of the country
and lasting memorials of its more perishable features.
He was born at Manchester
and died at Ambleside
on the 29th day of April 1823 in the 63rd year of his age
deeply lamented by a numerous family
and universally respected.
His afflicted widow
caused this stone to be erected."

The epitaph, is near the east end of the church in the churchyard at Grasmere. His wife was buried beside him ten years later and a daughter, Elizabeth, and son William had already been buried there.

*William Green's*
*Tombstone*
*in Grasmere*
*Churchyard.*

*Below:*
*The same stone*
*and that*
*of his wife,*
*daughter & son.*

# *Appendix IV*
# *Bibliography*

BEARD GEOFFREY. (1978) *The Greater House in Cumbria* (Westmorland Gazette)

BOUCH, C. M. L. & JONES, C.P. (1961) *The Lakes Counties 1500-1830. A social and economic history.* Manchester U.P.

BUDWORTH, JOSEPH. (1792) *A fortnight's Ramble to the Lakes in Westmoreland, Lancashire and Cumberland by a Rambler.* J. Nichols. London.

CLAY, ROTHA MARY. (1948) *Julius Caesar Ibbetson 1759-1817* (Country Life Ltd. London)

FOSKETT, DAPHNE (1974) *John Harden of Brathay Hall 1772-1847* Abbot Hall, Kendal.

GILPIN, THE REV. WILLIAM (1786) *Observations relative chiefly to Picturesque Beauty, made in the year 1772 on Several Parts of England; particularly the Mountains and Lakes of Cumberland and Westmorland.* London.

HILL, ALAN G. arranged and edited (1978) *The Letters of William and Dorothy Wordsworth.* Vols I, II, & III, O.U.P.

HOUSMAN, JOHN. (1800) *A topographical discription of Cumberland, Westmoreland, Lancashire and a part of the West Riding of Yorkshire.* Carlisle.

HUGHES, EDWARD. (1965) *North Country Life in the 18th century.* O.U.P.

HUTCHINSON, WILLIAM. (1776) *An excursion to the Lakes in Westmoreland and Cumberland; with a Tour through part of the Northern Counties, in the Years 1773 and 1774* J. Wilkie. London.

NICHOLSON, JOSEPH, & BURN, RICHARD, LL.D. (1777) *The History and Antiquities of the counties of Westmorland and Cumbria.* Strahan and Cadell. London.

RAWNSLEY, H. D. (1911), *By Fell and Dale at the English Lakes.* James MacLehose and Sons. Glasgow.

WEST, THOMAS. (1778) *A Guide to the Lakes, in Cumberland, Westmorland and Lancashire.* Kendal.

WORDSWORTH, WILLIAM. (1810) anonymously in Rev. Joseph Wilkinson's *Selected Views in Cumberland, Westmorland & Lancashire.*

WORDSWORTH, WILLIAM. (1820) *A Topographical Description of the Country of the Lakes, In the North of England.* Longman, Hurst, Rees, Orme and Brown. London.

ABBOT HALL, Exhibition Catalogue (1982) *Julius Caesar Ibbetson 1759-1817.*

ABBOT HALL, Exhibition Catalogue (1980) *The Viewfinders.*

READING MUSEUM & ART GALLERY Catalogue (1981) *William Havell 1782-1857.*

*As the Diaries are not yet transcribed for public study, specific references have not been given.*

# Illustrations

# Index